FROM **FUTURECASTING** TO **PRODUCT INNOVATION**

HOW TO FIND TOMORROW'S MOST PROMISING MARKETS AND CREATE PRODUCTS THAT PEOPLE WANT

GUERRIC DE TERNAY

From Futurecasting to Product Innovation
by Guerric de Ternay

Copyright © 2018-2024 Guerric de Ternay

All rights reserved.

Copyright encourages authors to take the time and effort necessary to create great work. It is what fuels the creative industry.

Thank you for buying an authorised edition of this book and for complying with copyright laws by not reproducing, adapting, scanning, or distributing any part of it in any form without permission.

Author name: Guerric de Ternay

Title: **From Futurecasting to Product Innovation: How to Find Tomorrow's Most Promising Markets and Create Products That People Want**

FOREWORD:

The opportunity and the value proposition

For more than a decade, I've been passionate about two of the most crucial questions that are at the heart of starting a new company or launching a new product. These are: (1) What market opportunity should you go after? and (2) What value proposition should you design?

Over the years, I've helped dozens of clients from aspiring entrepreneurs to Fortune 500 companies to answer these two questions. I've also answered these questions repeatedly for GoudronBlanc, a fashion brand I started in 2011. And I've done it enough times to learn one big lesson: These two questions are deceptively simple, but incredibly difficult to answer correctly. Getting them right requires a deep understanding of how the market is changing, what your customers want, and how to create your own secret sauce that competitors won't be able to copy. Easier said than done.

In this book bundle, I present all the tools I've developed to give a structure that can help you answer these two questions. I'm very excited about combining *The Opportunity Lenses* and *The Value Mix* into one overarching book that gives you the trajectory to go from exploring possible market opportunities to designing a product or a service to win in the most promising market.

With *The Opportunity Lenses*, you'll delve into foresight methods for identifying emerging trends and finding potential market opportunities. With *The Value Mix*, you'll explore a way to think about how to address unmet customer needs and create products that people want—what I call in the book your audience and your proposition.

This toolkit isn't a magic solution. If there's one truth in new venture building and product development, it's that every opportunity is unique. There's no textbook answer to launching a new business or a new product. But being equipped with the right tools can give you a clear advantage. Through real-world examples, practical exercises, and reflective questions, this book will challenge you to think differently about your business strategy and product design. You'll learn not just to adapt to market trends but to anticipate and shape them, setting the stage for sustainable growth.

So, as you turn these pages, keep an open mind and be ready to challenge your assumptions.

Enjoy the read!

To those who tirelessly do their bits to make a positive change in the lives of others.

TABLE OF CONTENTS

THE OPPORTUNITY LENSES

Introduction 4
CHAPTER ONE: What's an opportunity? 9
CHAPTER TWO: The Opportunity Mindset 17
CHAPTER THREE: Where opportunities come from 23
CHAPTER FOUR: Forces of change 35
CHAPTER FIVE: Zoom on Culture & Technology 43
CHAPTER SIX: Diffusion of change 59
CHAPTER SEVEN: Foresight 71
CHAPTER EIGHT: Opportunity Triggers 111
CHAPTER NINE: How to decide 147
CONCLUSION 178

THE VALUE MIX

Introduction 183
PART ONE Creating Value 189
PART TWO Understanding Your Audience 195
  CHAPTER ONE: Your Audience 197
  CHAPTER TWO: Context 199
  CHAPTER THREE: Goals 205
  CHAPTER FOUR: Worldviews 213
  CHAPTER FIVE: Concerns 223
PART THREE Shaping Your Proposition 227
  CHAPTER SIX: Your proposition 229

CHAPTER SEVEN: Alternatives *231*
CHAPTER EIGHT: Feature + Benefits *237*
CHAPTER NINE: Positioning *247*
CHAPTER TEN: Customer Experience + User Experience *257*

Book 1

THE
OPPORTUNITY LENSES

HOW TO SPOT YOUR NEXT BIG BUSINESS OPPORTUNITIES

Introduction

A VUCA environment

If you attend a lecture on strategy at a top business school, you'll likely hear the acronym "VUCA". The concept of VUCA was first used in 1987 by the US military education to explain the Volatility, Uncertainty, Complexity, and Ambiguity of the world at the time. Since the 2000s, business school professors have been using that notion because VUCA also reflects the reality of the business environment. It captures the new nature of business: The increased speed of change, the high level of unpredictability, the extreme intricacy of events (globally, locally, and across industries), and the likelihood for misinterpretation of what is happening.

Indeed, the business world has been changing in an accelerated way over the last few decades. Today, things that didn't seem even possible feel normal. It's acceptable to work 5 days a week from home. You won't be surprised if you hear that a 14-year-old YouTuber has negotiation power over a large corporate. The smartphone in your pocket has over 100,000 times the processing power of the computer that landed Neil Armstrong, Michael Collins, and Buzz Aldrin on the moon in 1969. Electric car adoption has been reaching an unprecedented level. And the fact that the parody of Bitcoin based on a meme that features a Shiba Inu dog called Dogecoin has reached nearly €100 billion of market value doesn't sound abnormal.

The pace of change speeds up every year. Technology and cultural shifts appear to spread nearly overnight. This new paradigm made old-school business tools such as strategic planning feel outdated. Companies are now required to adapt quickly. They need to be more flexible and embrace change faster in order to mimic the world's continuous and accelerated evolution. To remain fit for the future, companies must adopt ways of working that help their teams get better at identifying the next big opportunities and respond to market changes, to the democratisation of new technology, and to the intensifying competition.

These growing needs led to the creation of a range of "agile" and "human-centred" business toolkits that came from the worlds of software engineering and design. The lean startup, customer development, and design thinking are methodologies that have been helping companies get better at innovating. These techniques are now widely popular and used by startups as well as large corporations.

Your innovation process isn't enough

A process gives structure to how you pursue innovation. It maps the different activities, the governance, and the structure of the team you need to find opportunities and invent new products and business models. They can indicate criteria for making decisions to pursue or pivot, how to make sure to adopt a human-centred approach, and how long each phase should last. But all of this is limited to guiding the way, not the content and thinking that you need to innovate.

This creates a whole set of issues that I have observed by working with startups as well as Fortune 500 companies. The biggest problem is the confusion between an "idea" and an "opportunity". People tend to jump straight to ideas and overlook the necessary steps of considering opportunities first. It's one of the reasons why we see so many ideas that fall flat and fail.

Opportunities are a key ingredient of innovation. Whether you're an entrepreneur, an investor, or a leader in a company, you need a certain degree of innovation and, so, you need to be good at spotting opportunities.

Learning how to see through the fog

This book has the ambition to help you spot opportunities to create change in people's lives and, as a consequence, to capture value for your company.

If you want to identify new opportunities, you need to get better at noticing things and decoding the forces that shape and reshape the business environment. Finding opportunities is the result of continuous inquiries. It's about paying attention to what's surrounding you with a clear goal: To make sense of what is happening and discovering how you and your company can play a role in new emerging spaces.

For that, I have built a directory of what I call "lenses". These are a series of business tools that will help you notice changes in the world, explore the future, identify potential opportunities, and select the ones your company should pursue.

There isn't a set way of spotting opportunities. By definition, an opportunity depends on an ever-changing reality. And this reality has an impact that is different for every company. So, what I want to give you in this book is a set of business tools that can be adapted to your unique situation. The lenses should allow you to spot big business opportunities, no matter the kind of external circumstances you're facing or the type of company that you're part of.

A practical and inspiring read

The Opportunity Lenses is designed to provide you with guidance and food for thoughts. It isn't a textbook because there isn't a secret recipe that could work for everyone. The point isn't to hand you a user manual to follow, it's to empower you and your team with the right level of insight on what you need to identify and choose the next big opportunities for your company.

For me, "success" means that this book triggers discussions with your team, challenges how you currently do things, and encourages you to set up your own way of scouting for new opportunities. You shouldn't feel stuck in a process. Instead, this book should unlock new ways of looking at the world, at the future, and at the strategy of your company.

To achieve that, I have spiced up every lesson with business stories. I tried hard to share examples you would not have heard of before. I also wanted to avoid mentioning the GAMA (Google, Apple, Meta, Amazon), but there were instances where it was just relevant to tell a story that involves one of them in order to help me make a point more memorable. One would rightly reject a business book that mentions too many times Apple and Amazon as proof for a theory or as models to follow. These companies are more outliers than the norm. So, every time you see them in a story, remember that my point isn't to use it as evidence. The stories in this book are here to inspire you and help you remember each lens. They are used to make it stick by bringing more tangibility to what I want to share with you.

I'd like to finish the introduction with a piece of advice to make the most of reading The Opportunity Lenses. Before you start the book, decide that you will change three things in the way you do things in your work. As you're reading, find these three things. Write them down on Post-it notes or on a physical or digital notebook. And discuss them with your team to see how you can implement them. By setting the goal to take action and implement what you've read and found insightful, you'll make the most from diving into this book.

Now that you're ready, let's start!

CHAPTER ONE:

What's an opportunity?

Before we start, I want to make sure you and I are on the same page. So, we need to align on some basic definitions, especially on the meaning of "opportunity". Let's do this first step together by looking at this through the lexical lens.

A short definition

An opportunity is a set of circumstances that opens the door for you to make something that will create value for others, so that you may get a profitable return in exchange.

To make something that will create value for others, you'll need to invest your money, time, attention, and effort. If you do so, you will certainly expect to make some money in return—at least at some point.

To make a profitable return, you must therefore find ways to deliver value to your potential customers at a cost that is less than what they are willing to pay in exchange for the value you're creating for them.

Opportunities connect the dots

An opportunity is a moment when you see the potential conjunction of three things:

1. A *market*: a big enough audience of people or businesses who need or want something
2. A *value proposition*: a product or service that can offer what the audience needs or wants
3. A *profitable strategy*: a way to sell and deliver the proposition profitably

It means seeing the *possibilities* of creating a system where you can buy low and sell high, because someone or an organisation will benefit from what you'll be selling.

Opportunities aren't ideas

There's a lot of confusion between ideas and opportunities... An opportunity isn't a product or a business idea. It is a set of circumstances that opens the door to the success of potential ideas.

The idea is what you'd like to do. The opportunity is the reason why this could be a good idea.

Here's an example:

Over the last sixty years, more and more people have moved to cities. This has dramatically changed how they live. People who live in cities naturally adopt a more sedentary lifestyle. But at the same time, they still have a big appetite to exercise and move around.

Some entrepreneurs spotted the opportunity and went for it. It led to some pretty cool ideas: Nike (running in the 60s), Patagonia (rock climbing in the 70s), and Lululemon (yoga in the 90s).

Opportunities don't last forever

Some opportunities just last for a few months.

Do you remember, in 2017, when fidget spinners were trendy? Many online shops popped up. Months later, they were all gone.

Some opportunities have more longevity.

For example, there has been a mix of interesting circumstances for mobility services in cities. It's difficult or expensive to get around in most big cities (e.g., San Francisco, New York, and London). And since 2008, more and more people have smartphones. The combination of new technology and an ongoing mobility problem has opened the door to new ways to get around (e.g., ride-hailing and e-bikes). This was the case in 2008. And it still seems to be the case in 2021. But not everywhere…

That's because opportunities don't last forever.

As the mobility sector becomes more mature in cities, the circumstances change making the opportunities less and less interesting to go after. Indeed, a better public transport infrastructure is being set up, more competitors are offering solutions to get around, and so people are less and less interested in using new services.

And sometimes, the opportunity gets totally wiped out.

Video clubs, analogue photography, internet cafés were all the results of big opportunities. But changes in technology and culture made them disappear.

Opportunities are based on the future

A good opportunity isn't just about what the market wants now. It's too short term, which doesn't justify investing your time, money, and energy.

To be worth pursuing, an opportunity must have longevity. It means that you have identified fundamentals that encourage you to believe that, in the future, you'll be able to continue to make something that creates value for others, so that you may get a profitable return in exchange.

This requires you to get a deep understanding of how your market and your industry are likely to evolve in the future. It'll sound clearer after you've read the coming chapters—especially chapter 7.

Opportunities aren't certain

Choosing to go after an opportunity means taking some risks. This is inherent to doing something new. By definition, it might not work.

But not all opportunities are equal. Some opportunities are long shots that have a big potential, which comes at the cost of a high level of uncertainty. Others seem like safer options—but with limited returns. It's rare to encounter an opportunity that has no risk *and* that can offer a high return on investment.

Here are examples of risks you may have to face:

- *Marketing risks* – Can you get enough people to buy and use your product or service?
- *R&D risks* – Can the proposition be built at the right cost?
- *Financial risks* – Can you secure the resources necessary to go after the opportunity?
- *Organisational risks* – Will the team be able to deliver this?
- *Competition risks* – Will the competition intensify and create pressure on pricing?
- *Macro risks* – Will this business model win in the future macroeconomics environment?

The good thing is that you can gain confidence over time.

You can't control all the risks. But you can evaluate them and de-risk an opportunity by experimenting, learning more about the market, the R&D process, the people involved, the competition, etc.

You'll never know for sure. There will always be this element of "it might not work". But as you gradually commit, the level of certainty will grow. This may reinforce your confidence, making you realise that you were right. Or this may require you to pivot your strategy because you originally made the wrong assumptions. In any case, you must remain flexible in how you pursue an opportunity.

Opportunities may be influenced

There's a tension between what you can influence and what you can't. It's rare to be able to create new opportunities from scratch. Even the Coca-Colas, the Facebooks, and the Googles of this world struggle to do so. But it's possible to influence an opportunity to make it bigger.

Here's an example:

A lot of people have become real aficionados of sneakers. They buy expensive shoes; collect those shoes; and even queue to get the latest models. There are many reasons that can explain the sneakerhead movement. But here, I want to focus on how some brands have been able to grow that movement.

Nike and Adidas were well-positioned to influence the opportunity. They were established leaders in selling sports shoes. This allowed them to see early that sneakers weren't just about sports, but also fashion and culture. Instead of being anchored in their own world of "we're a sports brand", they decided to go after this new growth opportunity for their brands. And they did everything they could to make the opportunity even bigger, e.g., hiring talented designers, launching provocative sneakers, creating limited editions, collaborating with other brands and celebrities, etc.

It's unlikely that the inception of the opportunity was in their control. When the whole streetwear trend started, Nike and Adidas were very much focusing on creating sports shoes, clothes, and equipment. But they were fast to react and did the right things to be part of the streetwear trend and amplify the sneakerhead movement.

Opportunities are subjective

A good opportunity for you may not be a good one for me. A good opportunity for Heineken isn't necessarily a good opportunity for a local brewery—and vice versa.

Your company won't always have a right to play. An opportunity could be too small for a large corporate and right for a small or medium company. Maybe it doesn't fit the overall strategic direction of the business. Or, maybe there are too many competitors that are better positioned to go after the opportunity.

Not everyone is equal in front of the same opportunity. There are many factors to take into account, e.g., size, location, resources, capabilities, current strategy, brand values, and expected ROI. I go into more detail in chapter 9, which is about how to decide on what opportunities your company should pursue.

Opportunities require commitment

Going after any opportunity requires you to commit resources such as money, efforts, time, and energy. You'll need to build a team, create or buy assets, develop a proposition, and find ways to deliver it profitably.

Obviously, you shouldn't go all-in before you've gained confidence that it's the right thing for your company. You need to de-risk your investment. Go step by step. Committing can be done through *gradual* commitment.

When you face a potential opportunity, dig into the hypotheses you're making: *What needs to be true for this opportunity to be interesting and relevant for your company?*

Test these hypotheses. Talk to potential customers. Show them prototypes. Build a back-of-the-envelope draft of your P&L. Do everything you can to learn more about the factors that will allow you to be more confident about the decision to commit additional resources to go after the opportunity. At each stage, it should be easier and easier for the decision-makers in the company to commit more resources.

Opportunities need a dose of focus

Focus is about setting priorities and avoiding getting distracted by other options. When you decide to pursue an opportunity, you make the choice to allocate resources to this project, and say "no" to all the other possible opportunities. This is the essence of what "strategy" means.

Saying "yes" to an opportunity has a cost. The opportunity cost represents the potential gain you miss out on when choosing one opportunity over other options. The cost of opening one door is that it closes all the other doors.

However, focus doesn't mean being locked into a decision.

You may want to find ways to leave room for reconsidering your options later. Sometimes, a new opportunity arises unexpectedly, or you hit a challenge that you didn't anticipate. It's important to find the right balance between focus and optionality.

Opportunities may be hard to see

Spotting opportunities is about how you look at things. And if you want to see what may be hard to see, you need to be in the right frame of mind.

It's the story of the hammer and the nail; someone with a hammer sees nails to hit everywhere they look. Or it's the story of the red car; once you own a red car, you see red cars all the time.

The challenge is that, sometimes, you have a hammer in your hand. So you see nails everywhere, but you should be looking for screws.

The same happens when you're looking for new opportunities. You may be looking for the next big thing, but you should be looking for incremental growth. Or you may want to play it safe with minimum investment, while it's the right time to take risks.

CHAPTER TWO:

The Opportunity Mindset

To find new opportunities, you must have the right business toolkit, i.e., what I've called "your opportunity lenses". But it's only one part of the trick. Let's see what's needed on top of having the right lenses.

It's about the way you think

> "When the winds of change blow, some people build walls and others build windmills."
>
> – CHINESE PROVERB

Your way of thinking will influence what you're able to see. Even if you're using the right lens, you may miss what's to be seen because you don't have the appropriate mindset. But what does that mean?

Two jobs especially require adopting the opportunity mindset: investor and entrepreneur.

People in those jobs tend to be quite optimistic. They see opportunities when it seems that things are going badly. Through their eyes, a crisis can easily become a fertile ground for setting up something new and exciting.

What most investors and entrepreneurs have in common is that they are curious, rigorous, quick to respond, and proactively trying new things. They're constantly seeking new opportunities, willing to do what they can to get things moving in the right direction, and ready to act when something relevant comes up.

Their mindset allows them to see what others aren't seeing.

Beginner forever

> *"In the beginner's mind, there are many possibilities, in the expert's mind there are few."*
>
> – SHUNRYU SUZUKI, ZEN MONK

The beginner's mind refers to an attitude of openness. When you are a beginner, you barely know anything. You keep an open mind and actively seek information. You're constantly exploring.

Think about a baby who sees something for the first time. They'll touch it, put it in the mouth, throw it in the air. They have no preconception. They are openly exploring.

Or think about when you travel to a country you have never visited before. You see new fashion styles, you try new food, you discover new places, and you experience new traditions. You keep being curious about everything that's happening around you.

It's a sense of wonder and fascination that leads you to repetitively ask: "what is happening?" and "why is that?".

But as you learn and build expertise, you naturally explore less. You start anticipating what may happen. You "know that already". You've "seen it before". You're less open to seeing the new. You're losing the intense curiosity that was pushing you to seek information.

Expertise can be a trap. So as you become more knowledgeable, you need to pay attention even more than before. You feel familiar with what you're seeing, so you need to intentionally push yourself to keep your beginner's eyes wide open to spot what's new and important. You need to find ways to make "familiar" seem "strange".

An attentive expert

> *"An expert is a man who has made all the mistakes which can be made, in a narrow field."*
>
> – NIELS BOHR, Danish Physicist

Being curious isn't enough. There's no point in being extra naive and trying to reinvent the wheel. You need some foundational knowledge too. You must be or become an "expert".

What sets experts apart is their ability to make quick hypotheses about what's going on. They can identify patterns in what would seem random or confusing to people who are less familiar with the subject matter.

Observe traders looking at charts. What you see are lines moving in a disorganised way. What they see are price trends, support and resistance levels, momentum indicators, etc. They can even get a feel for other traders' emotions.

If you've never seen a trader, then think about a professional chess player. For them, each move has a meaning and takes part in a complex system. When they look at a chessboard, they see things that you won't see.

Experts can make sense of what's happening, even if it appears chaotic at first glance.

Looking at things as both a beginner and an expert will give you:

- An eager desire to explore and learn;
- An ability to make sense of an avalanche of data.

And this will help you identify the changes that trigger new opportunities.

Proactively experimenting

> *"Observation is a passive science, experimentation an active science."*
>
> – CLAUDE BERNARD, French Psychologist

The risk with opportunities is to get stuck in a mode of analysis paralysis.

You're not sure. You're afraid of making the wrong decision. You're trying to see if the return on investment for seizing the opportunity is worth the risk. You prefer to wait and see. You can't decide to commit and just decide to do more research and more planning.

Analysis paralysis is a vicious circle. It's a symptom of lack of confidence, or something that's less talked about in the business world: "fear".

One solution to gain confidence is to try it out yourself—to experiment.

Experimenting means: Starting small; progressively buying confidence that it's something that could work; testing assumptions; de-risking big investments; iterating as you learn.

Big businesses tend to struggle with this mindset. They like to plan in advance. They ask for clarity on how things will change over the next five years. They want everything to fit in a tidy spreadsheet model or a clear roadmap.

But you can't reach perfect certainty in a model. There are too many variables, too much nuance, and so many assumptions baked in. This is where experimentation comes in handy.

It's about being hypothesis-driven.

Here's what your reflex should be when an opportunity seems appealing but still uncertain. Highlight what you don't know, be clear on your assumptions, and progressively gain confidence by testing your hypotheses.

This hypothesis-driven mindset can help you gain the confidence you need before committing to bigger investments.

Prepared mind

"Chance favours the prepared mind."
— LOUIS PASTEUR, French Scientist

To spot and pursue an opportunity, it's important to find yourself in the right place at the right time (often with the right people). For that, you must be ready to make a move when needed.

I'm not talking about naive excitement for the latest hype. It rarely pays out to be in a hurry. But you also want to avoid being too slow. It is common to see companies focusing so much on doing thorough market research that by the time they feel ready to make a move all of their competitors have already jumped in.

To be quick to respond, you must feel prepared. Here are some things that help:

- Being aligned on what you stand for, and what you don't stand for,
- Having the ability to experiment and gradually de-risk opportunities,
- Building a flexible and lean decision-making process,
- Having the guts to go after opportunities that may require to reinvent yourself in the future—as they say: "what got you here won't get you there",
- Keeping your eyes wide open as to what is changing in the lives of your customers.

Before getting in the starting block, ready to go after an opportunity that seems right for your company, you must be geared up with the appropriate mindset and your opportunity lenses. Let's have a look at those lenses. Shall we?

CHAPTER THREE:

Where opportunities come from

If you want to see something that's ephemeral, you need to anticipate how it's going to appear and grow. Opportunities come and go. And to spot them before they go, you must have an understanding of where they come from. Let's approach this with an evolutionary lens.

The short story

If nothing is happening, there's no story to be told. For a good story, you need something new that creates friction and disrupts the life of the main character.

There are two typical plots in a novel:

1. A person goes on a journey;
2. A stranger comes to town.

Both situations lead to an interesting storyline because something new is happening. And this event changes the life of the main character.

The Story Arc

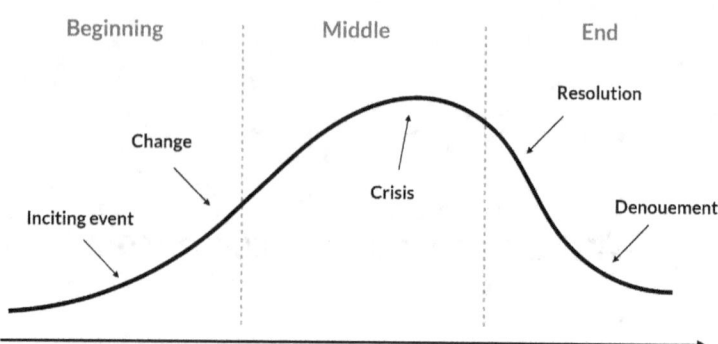

It's the same for opportunities. An opportunity is the result of something new happening in the business environment or in the company.

Imbalance

An opportunity arises when there is a gap between what someone wants and what is available to them.

There's an imbalance in the market because:

- On one hand, someone has a problem to solve or wants a better way to achieve their goals; something doesn't feel right for them.

- On the other hand, new solutions could be available to make their lives better; but these aren't accessible yet.

This imbalance between demand and supply triggers the opportunity.

Change

Opportunities come from both change and lack of change happening. You can notice some imbalance when something has changed but the rest hasn't. This creates tension. There's a gap between what people want and what can be done for them.

This change can be a shift in what people need and want, or a shift in what businesses can do and offer to create value. For example:

- People's expectations have changed, but what's available for them to buy hasn't changed yet. Or people have a new problem because something has changed in their lives, but nothing is addressing their new problem yet.
- New technology has made it possible to adopt a new business model, but the companies in the industry haven't yet changed.

When something changes, it creates some imbalance in the market. This is what triggers the opportunity. Then, companies adapt and things settle—until something changes again.

Hard to control

> *"The chief task in life is simply this: to identify and separate matters so that I can say clearly to myself which are externals not under my control, and which have to do with the choices I actually control."*
>
> – EPICTETUS, Greek Stoic Philosopher

Change is continuous. So, new opportunities will keep coming up, while others will fade away. Without getting too philosophical here, there's a sense of flow that businesses have to embrace. Change happens at its own pace.

At a macro level, there's little you can control. Even companies like Ford, Google, Shell, or Airbnb don't have any control over a pandemic, an economic crisis, cultural shifts, or the inevitable development of new technologies.

Though, what you can do is to identify these changes early, get clear on their implications, and use that thinking to spot new opportunities for your company.

Crisis

A crisis is the quintessential moment of change. It is "change" on steroids. It refers to both:

- a situation of instability;
- a turning point when the situation before doesn't look like the situation after.

The difficulties, the danger, and the uncertainty, which are triggered by a crisis, have the power to rapidly transform social norms (how people see and assess things) and behaviours (what people do). This rapid—often brutal—change is a catalyst for new big opportunities.

The financial crisis of 2007–2008 created an unprecedented shift towards freelancing and micro-entrepreneurship. Millions of unfortunate people lost their jobs. Then, it unexpectedly became more acceptable for them to hustle and run their own micro-businesses. Climbing the corporate ladder wasn't the only path anymore. This radical cultural change created new opportunities to build businesses that support freelancers. And a number of freelancing platforms popped up, e.g., 99designs, Freelancer.com, Toptal, Fiverr, and Contently (among others).

At the moment when I'm writing these pages, we are in 2020–2021. The world is going through a global sanitary crisis. This is a major event that has pushed the adoption of new social and cultural norms. As we've experienced it already, the COVID crisis—and the resulting imbalances—created massive new business opportunities, allowing people to work, live, shop, and socialise in new ways.

A market reset

> *"Looking at what happened to print advertising after 2009 and [I] wonder if that [will] repeat. A*

crash can be a market reset. You don't return to the old normal afterwards, but make a new normal. Everyone rethinks their budgets."

– BENEDICT EVANS, Independent Analyst

Not all shifts are equal. The intensity varies from slow incremental change to a total reset of the market.

Incremental change looks like this: We've experienced a gradual shift towards more socially and environmentally sustainable products. To most, it may feel that sustainability has become an important topic in recent years. But in reality, the concept of socially responsible and eco-friendly products was already talked about in the 1960s. The first fair trade certification appeared in the 1980s. Ecover, a Belgian company that manufactures eco-friendly cleaning products, was created in 1979. Today, every company claims that they want to act more sustainably in the way they operate. But it's taken decades for sustainability to become mainstream. This is incremental change.

A market reset happens when the market dynamics are entirely reshuffled. Incumbents lose their competitive advantages; the value chain is being redefined; and any player can reimagine the role that they play in the business environment.

A good example of a market reset is what happened to the music industry in the early 2000s, when the value chain was totally disrupted by the move from CDs to digital audio formats. Selling CDs was a very profitable business to be in. Everyone, from the music labels to the stores, was making a decent living out of this—until the landscape dramatically changed. In just a few years, people stopped buying CDs and started downloading audio files or using streaming services such as Apple Music (formerly iTunes), Spotify, and YouTube. This was a total market reset for the labels, the musicians, and the music stores. The value chain changed and every player had to adapt—without having a word to say about whether they wanted things to change.

When thinking about change, there are two important

questions you can ask yourself: *"How big will the shift be?"* and *"How fast will it happen?"*. I'll dive more into these questions in the following chapters.

Adapting

> *"The greatest danger in times of turbulence is not the turbulence—it is to act with yesterday's logic."*
>
> – PETER DRUCKER, Management Consultant

The stock market crashed at the end of February 2020. This was mainly triggered by the rapid rise of the COVID pandemic. The unexpected event led Sequoia, a 50-year-old venture capital firm known for its early investments in Apple, CISCO, Google, Skyscanner, and Airbnb, to release a public note guiding founders and CEOs on how to ensure the health of their business.

Here's an extract of their note:

> *"Having weathered every business downturn for nearly fifty years, we've learned an important lesson — nobody ever regrets making fast and decisive adjustments to changing circumstances. In downturns, revenue and cash levels always fall faster than expenses. In some ways, business mirrors biology. As Darwin surmised, those who survive "are not the strongest or the most intelligent, but the most adaptable to change."*

Their key message was: "Adapt to change".

"Adaptation" is the process of adjusting to suit a new situation or changing environment. It requires to be aware of what's changing, spot the potential threats, and identify what are the opportunities that emerge from this new forming landscape.

It happens to see large corporations dramatically adapt their main business model. In the early 1900s, Nintendo sold cards in Japan. In the 1970s, Nintendo pivoted its business and started making video games. Before it became a car manufacturer, Peugeot was a steel foundry and a saw maker. The company was also known for its famous pepper grinders.

Threats vs. Opportunities

> *"Creativity is just connecting things. Innovation is the ability to see change as an opportunity—not a threat."*
>
> – STEVE JOBS, Co-founder, Apple

A threat can also be an opportunity. I know… It's easy to say it's just a matter of perspective. If change puts your current business model at risk, your gut feeling will be to treat this change as a threat. Everything was working as planned, and something you didn't want to happen is about to disturb everything. Aouch!

Change is a threat to the status quo. But if you can adapt rapidly, change can be an opportunity to gain an edge.

Here's an example:

When Netflix realised that streaming had the potential to take over DVD renting, they forced themselves to adapt their business model.

Technology fundamentally changed the way people could watch movies. They didn't need a DVD anymore. They could directly stream movies and series online. This technological change was a threat to Netflix's DVD rental business. But they treated the change as an opportunity to gain an advantage against other rental services. (I'm not saying it's easy and they won't say that either.)

Taken on time, change creates opportunities to adapt and gain an advantage against the competition. It pushes you to serve your customers better by rethinking your business model: who your target audience is, how you can create value for them, and how you should sell, operate your business, and allocate your resources.

If you can't adapt

"*Innovate or die*" is a buzz-phrase that has been used for decades as a threat to big businesses—and a way to sell consulting services.

But it's also a useful reminder that when the world is changing, you must also find a way to change. And innovating is the process of embracing or making change happen by creating something new.

It's what Schumpeter famously called "*creative destruction*", the process of "*mutation that incessantly revolutionises the economic structure from within, incessantly destroying the old one, incessantly creating a new one*". It's the destruction of underperforming business models and the creation of better-suited ones.

If you can't adapt, change will threaten your business. If you can adapt fast enough, change becomes a source of opportunities.

A new business model

> "*Progress is impossible without change, and those who cannot change their minds cannot change anything.*"
>
> – GEORGE BERNARD SHAW, Irish Playwright

Change threatens a company when its business model no longer suits the resulting business environment. To turn a threat into an opportunity, a company needs a new business model.

Put simply, to create a new business model, you have to adjust three key elements: who, what, and how.

- *Who* you sell to: your target audience
- *What* value you create for them: your proposition
- *How* you create and deliver that value: the value chain, your operational model

I simplified things here. But it's often helpful to go back to first principles. It helps get rid of a lot of the clutter created by the industry jargon. Have you ever summed up your company's business model in that way? *"Who do we want as customers? What value do we create for them? How do we make this happen?"*

Why change?

> *"Change is hard because people overestimate the value of what they have and underestimate the value of what they may gain by giving that up."*
>
> – JAMES A. BELASCO, Business Author

Why does an entrepreneur decide to start a business? Why would a company decide to change its business model?

It may be a necessity. They could lose something. If they don't adapt, they'll take the risk of becoming irrelevant.

Or it may be a way to create additional gains. They see that they can create and capture more value by pursuing a new opportunity. Here's an example:

The energy drink sector is dominated by giants such as Red Bull, Monster, Coca-Cola, and Burn. It doesn't look like a market full of opportunity. But the founders of a startup company saw a change in the market. Indeed, people were starting to be interested in "natural" and "plant-based" ingredients. These people believed that all the dominant players were full of artificial additives. They wanted an energy drink that felt more natural.

Their idea was Tenzing, "*a plant-based energising drink with a triple hit of natural caffeine, vitamin C and electrolytes.*" According to the company, the drink is made with only a few ingredients that you can name without a degree in chemistry: "*Sparkling Water, Beet Sugar, Lemon Juice from concentrate, Green Tea, Indian Gooseberry, Guarana, Caffeine from Green Coffee, Himalayan Rock Salt.*"

A gap in the market triggered the opportunity. It was the right set of circumstances for a startup to go after it with the expectations to create additional gains.

Your response will create change too

There's a reason why your customers are buying into your proposition. It's because they believe that it will somewhat make their lives better. Even what appears to be the most elementary products or services are bought because they make a difference in people's lives.

Here's an example:

When I started GoudronBlanc in 2011, I was set to build a brand that specialises in making high-quality T-shirts for men. I wanted our customers to get the best T-shirts. Throughout the years, I learnt more about our customers and what they wanted. It made me realise that men don't go to GoudronBlanc.com just to buy great T-shirts. This is just what happens at the surface level.

Buying high-quality T-shirts is a proxy for something else. So, what's the real story? What they want is the excitement of receiving and unpacking a well-crafted product; the confidence of feeling great, as they wear clothes they're proud of wearing; a story to tell their friends about what they were; and, sometimes, the ability to make a thoughtful gift to someone else.

One of the things I prefer is talking with our customers to get a deeper understanding of the role that the GoudronBlanc T-shirts play in their lives. When you receive an email from a customer asking for guidance to find the right size because she wants to surprise her husband by getting him a couple of T-shirts after he mentioned GoudronBlanc several times, this makes you appreciate the change that a business can make.

A new product or service is the expression of a change you want to make in someone's life or in an organisation. It's an ideal (or at least a better situation) that you want to create for someone else. Going after an opportunity is taking the chance to make this change happen.

Two levels of change

You can observe change at two levels:

- At the macro level, you can see the big shifts that are shaping industries in the world or a country. I call them "forces of change" (chapter 4).
- At the micro level, you find circumstances that directly create new business opportunities. I use the phrase "opportunity triggers" (chapter 8).

The line between the two is blurred. But you understand that macro is the lens that means large scale and micro is the lens that is closer to what your business does. Both are useful to spot new opportunities.

CHAPTER FOUR:

Forces of change

Opportunities come from change in the marketplace. But how does this change manifest itself? What should you look at more specifically? Let's look at this through what I call the "STEER lenses".

Systemic change

Change is complex. The business environment is shaped by multiple forces. It's a whole system that is constantly moving and shifting. As they produce change, these forces play a role in the creation of new opportunities.

But there's a near infinity of elements that make the system evolve over time. It can be challenging to identify what forces you should pay attention to, and which are the ones that will have the biggest impact in creating new opportunities for your business.

So, in this chapter, I introduce a framework that will help you see through the complexity and identify more clearly the major forces of change.

STEER

The acronym "STEER" refers to a set of lenses that will help you organise your thinking when you want to understand what is changing in your sector.

STEER stands for:

- Socio-cultural,
- Technological,
- Economic,
- Environmental, and
- Regulatory.

These are the main five forces of change that shape the environment in which your company operates. Using the framework will help you make sense of the type of change you are facing and better understand where new opportunities are coming from.

Each area has its own set of players and stakeholders. Change among these is measured differently. You don't assess regulatory changes in the same way you would research socio-cultural changes. Breaking change down into these five categories will help you in noticing specific trends and signals that could be interesting for spotting opportunities.

In the following chapters, I will share with you a model to visualise how change spreads over time (chapter 6), and a process for forming a point of view on how change could impact your business environment (chapter 7). Before that, I'd like to dive into the distinctions among the five forces of change.

Socio-cultural

"Socio-cultural" encompasses change related to group dynamics as well as individual behaviours. It's about how people live, where they live, how they socialise, how they shop, how they work, and what they believe.

It includes changes in demography, education, religion, social norms, lifestyle, holiday routine, leisure activities and hobbies, income distribution, social mobility, spending and saving habits, life stages, family life, housing choices, urban/rural divide, work-life, corporate culture, etc.

An example:

The way people work has been changing a lot in the last decade. Since the 2010s, more and more people have been able to work remotely. And in 2020, the trend accelerated to reach 20-40% of the population working up to 5 days a week from home.

In 2015–2016, my job gave me the chance to work remotely, so I decided to spend a year working while travelling around the world. When I explained that to people, it was hard for many of them to take me seriously. They didn't understand how you could get work and travel at the same time. Now, most people who have experienced being able to work from home could get their head around this.

What I did is often called being a digital nomad. This phenomenon has been an interesting signal of the future impact of remote working. The movement started in the late 1990s thanks to new technologies offering the ability to work and collaborate remotely. If you don't have to go to the office every day, this allows you to live wherever you want, or even constantly be on the move. You can live in the countryside or go travelling.

The ability to work from anywhere and its recent wide acceptance is a major socio-cultural shift. It will continue to have strong implications on where people decide to live, whether they should rent or buy, the types of jobs that they want to do, etc. I'm genuinely interested to see all the opportunities that this new paradigm creates.

Technological

Technology is what enables businesses to create and deliver value to their customers.

"Technological" covers changes in science, medicine, engineering, computing, hardware and software, tools and machinery, cost and speed of development, processes and methodologies, energy sources, telecommunication and connectivity, media formats, intellectual property, product lifecycles, venture capital investments, R&D investments, etc.

An example:

The development of the iPhone and Android smartphones triggered a significant technological shift. One key feature was the ability to get instant geolocation.

The new technology created a lot of opportunities for map applications (e.g., Google Maps, Waze, and CityMapper), ride-hailing services (e.g., Uber and Bolt), food delivery (e.g., Deliveroo and JustEat), and even video games (e.g., Pokemon Go).

Economic

"Economic" refers to changes that impact the economy, i.e., all the activities related to production, trade, and consumption of goods and services.

These include the economic crisis but also changes in interest rate, inflation or deflation, exchange rate, real estate price, unemployment rate, industrial production, bankruptcies, consumer confidence, percentage of freelance workers, purchasing power, quality of life, productivity, GDP, number of companies incorporated, stock markets, oil price, electricity cost, etc.

An example:

I used to work with Estonian startups. The country is a vibrant hub for tech startups in Eastern Europe. What's interesting is one of the reasons Estonia has been able to build this startup ecosystem.

It's due to the success of a handful of companies: Playtech, Skype, and more recently TransferWise. As these companies grew, they built a pool of talented software engineers, attracted foreign investments, and brought attention to Estonia. Many Estonians found financial success and kept the money in the startup ecosystem by investing as business angels. From there, the Estonian ecosystem continued to grow.

The success of a handful of companies was a big enough change to create opportunities for many more startups at the country level.

Environmental

"Environmental" touches everything that concerns our surroundings as they are shaped by nature and human activity.

It encompasses topics such as pollution, reserves of raw materials, diseases, sanitary crisis, natural disasters, climate and meteorology, landscape transformation, water availability, air quality, waste management, etc.

These are very much influenced by urban activity, housing, transport, agriculture, mining, oil production, power generation, and manufacturing.

An example:

Disposable plastic products have been a growing source of pollution, especially in the ocean. Thanks to the work of a few charities, we are now more aware of this problem. Plastic pollution creates lots of issues. It spreads on the coasts, damages marine landscapes, and kills many types of fish and other species that ingest or are entangled by plastic debris.

This problem also became an opportunity for non-profit organisations (e.g., Parley) and fashion brands (e.g., Adidas). Parley and other partners collect the plastic from coastal areas. The plastic is sorted and shipped to factories, where it is upcycled and transformed into yarn fibres. These are then used to create new products such as Adidas sneakers.

This environmental change due to plastic pollution is way bigger than what Parley and Adidas can handle. Millions of tons of plastics end up in the ocean. Imagine the scale: A car weighs about 1.5 tons and is more compact than a plastic bottle. We're talking about millions of tons, this is a massive volume of plastics (from bottles to fishing nets to random plastic bags).

The organisations were able to reframe this global environmental change into a business opportunity that benefits the planet, their businesses, and their customers.

I mentioned Parley and Adidas, but many other organisations are doing some great things to respond to major environmental changes. Kudos to all of them!

Regulatory

"Regulatory" relates to how the government and other public bodies intervene in the economy and society by setting new laws and regulations.

This is about changes happening around political stability, healthcare, education system, public spending, foreign policy, tax policy, custom and trade barriers, subsidies, employment law, competition oversight, consumer law, health and safety regulations, criminal law, company law, intellectual property, accounting, etc.

Elections and other major political events are significant turning points, as they are likely to influence the adoption of new laws.

An example:

There's a tendency to focus on socio-cultural and technological changes (and I will do this in the next chapter). But, you shouldn't underestimate the potential of new regulations for creating opportunities.

Here's an example from the UK banking system:

Encouraged by the European payment regulation known as "PSD2", the UK has been trying to promote innovation by breaking down the banks' monopoly on their customers' data. This led to an initiative called "Open Banking", which pushes banks to make data easy to be shared across platforms when a customer requests it.

The Open Banking initiative has created opportunities for new financial services. Easy data sharing means that you can get a budgeting app to analyse your data so that it gives you insight into your spending patterns. It also means that it's easier for you to move from one bank to another, making it possible for challenger banks to compete with the larger institutions.

It's one thing to have an initiative that encourages making data shareable. It's another to have the infrastructure that facilitates secured data sharing across software solutions. This need for the right infrastructure was an opportunity that a startup named TrueLayer went after. The company positioned itself as a partner of choice for banks, financial services, and startups that all needed and wanted to make it easier for data to be securely shared.

This wasn't a customer need or some new technology that triggered the opportunity, but a change in regulation. The European PSD2 regulation initiated a change that made it possible for a company like TrueLayer to be started.

CHAPTER FIVE:

Zoom on Culture & Technology

Out of the five STEER forces, there are two I'd like to spend more time on: socio-cultural forces (which I will also call "culture" and "market") and technological forces (also called "technology" here).

Culture gives a sense of what people believe and the way they live. Ultimately, it shapes what people need and want.

Technology is the expression of how companies influence the other four forces. New technologies have an impact on socio-cultural, economic, environmental, and regulatory dynamics.

Let's use a magnifying lens to have a closer look at these two areas.

A big tension

I find fascinating the tension between "market pull" and "technology push". Is it an increase in demand from the market that leads to new opportunities? Or is it a change of technology and supply that creates new opportunities?

Obviously, you need both demand and supply—a seller and a buyer—to have an opportunity. But sometimes one predominates. And sometimes the other makes the difference.

"Supply-led innovation vs. demand-led innovation" is an endless debate.

You can argue that people don't know what they want. So, you need to invent something for people to realise that they want it. This is the infamous quote attributed to Henry Ford: *"If I had asked people what they wanted, they would have said faster horses."*

But you can also look at all these new inventions that never found any success. People didn't have the need or desire for a smart fork or a Segway. This one makes me think of the misleading adage: *"If you build it, they will come."* (Spoiler alert: they rarely do.)

Pulling and pushing

It's because of this tension between the market and technology that we talk about "pulling" and "pushing", i.e., is it the market or the technology that creates the opportunity?

Market pull

Market pull is about looking at opportunities through the lens of the needs and desires of a specific audience. It's like saying, "What can we do to better help them achieve their goals?"

It's the demand from the market that triggers new opportunities. So you want first to identify new needs and desires to decide that there's an opportunity for a new product and service.

Technology push

> *"If a man has good corn, or wood, or boards, or pigs, to sell, or can make better chairs or knives, crucibles or church organs, than anybody else, you will find a broad hard-beaten road to his house, though it be in the woods."*

– RALPH WALDO EMERSON, American Essayist

Technology push is driven by R&D. It's a solution in search of a problem. It's like saying, "We have this tool, what can we use it for?".

The opportunity comes from something new that we *can* do. It allows you to create a specific product or service that *may* be needed or wanted. It's based on the assumption that "if we make it, they will come".

In this case, the development of new technology creates the opportunity.

Technology/Market Fit

Pull and push must come together at some point for a business to work.

You can't build a business if you have a technology that no one wants, or a clear need with no feasible solution.

The distinction helps understand the dynamic of any specific sector:

- Are you more in a "pull sector" like healthcare, where the market needs medicine but has to wait for technology to change and make new treatments possible?
- Are you more in a "push sector" like fashion, where the creation and the supply of a new collection generate the demand for clothes?

You start seeing the full picture now. Market pull and technology push are two useful lenses to understand where new opportunities may come from:

- Through new needs, habits, and desires, the market is "pulling" new technology. It indicates clear demand for a product or a service. It's more like healthcare.

- Technology "pushes" the market. It creates new behaviours and makes the market aware of new needs and desires. It shapes our culture, what people believe, how they live, and what they want and need. It's more like fashion.

In most cases, there's more nuance between technology push and market pull. It's not all one or the other. But, it's still interesting to answer the following question: "Which is the one that is slightly outweighing the other one?"

Zoom on Technology

Technology is what businesses use and produce to create value. Tech doesn't have any feeling or emotion. So, we need both empathy and a method to figure out how it can best serve human needs and people's desires.

What can we do with it?

The technology/market fit always seems obvious in hindsight.

But the opportunity for new technology isn't always clear at first. This means that when some new technology is invented, it can sit around for a while before we find a good opportunity to use it.

Here's an example:

Electric air conditioning was originally invented to control the temperature and humidity in printing factories. The story says that it's when the plant owners saw the workers choosing to eat their lunch in the air-conditioned room that they understood there was another (and potentially bigger) opportunity.

It took years to figure out what to do with the air conditioning technology, something that seems obvious to us now.

Yesterday's tech questions:

- We have *fire*. What can we do with it?

- We have *steam*. What can we do with it?
- We have *electricity*. What can we do with it?
- We have *the Internet*. What can we do with it?
- We have *computers in our pockets*. What can we do with them?

Today's tech questions

- We have *augmented reality*. What can we do with it?
- We have *machine learning*. What can we do with it?
- We have *blockchain technology*. What can we do with it?

Building blocks

New technology is the result of building on existing technology.

Inventors and engineers don't like to start from scratch. They use existing methods, tools, and building blocks to create something new.

There's no point in "reinventing the wheel".

Even what has been considered as big tech revolutions were the result of bringing blocks together. The Internet, the iPhone, or Uber, none of these were made from scratch.

Technology is built by reusing what already exists to make new stuff—and hopefully stuff that people want.

Iterating

Technology is the result of trials and errors. New inventions are made by trying new things, failing, failing again, and one day reaching the vision you had in mind—or maybe didn't have in mind.

This is the infamous quote by Thomas Edison about

finding 10,000 ways not to create a light bulb—just trial and error. Iteration is the process through which we create new technology and improve it over time.

Sometimes, it's a startup trying to find its "product-market fit", sometimes it's a global macro-experiment like what's happening with augmented reality and blockchain.

Technology changes culture and business

> *"Successful innovators focused on technology as a driver of value, not just as a tool for operational efficiency."*
>
> – COSTAS MARKIDES,
> Professor, London Business School

Technology has this interesting ability to shape our culture by creating new habits and new ways of looking at things.

Think about how the business of sharing news has evolved:

It went from being shared by travellers at the pace of horse riding across the country to instant availability on the Internet.

- News used to spread as fast as people—or pigeons—could travel.
- Then, came the era of telegram and mass printing.
- In parallel, we saw the rise of radio news.
- TV took off a little bit later.
- Then, the Internet came and made news widely available almost instantaneously.
- And today, smartphones make it possible to get the news in any format, anywhere at any time.

It's a simplified chronology. But you can see how each step created new consumption habits. And in parallel, technology also shaped how reporting is done.

- My assumption is that travellers were rarely paid to share the news. Official statements were shared by civil servants. But, most news spread by word of mouth.
- When mass printing arrived, we needed professionals to report what was happening, to take photos, and to format all this information.
- Radio was another medium for sharing news. It still required reporters, but also a live presenter in a radio studio.
- TV made it possible to share video content—so you needed to add cameras and post-production into the mix.
- The Internet changed the news model again. It has opened the door to new types of reporting and given amateurs the ability to share news and analysis—without having to go through a big news outlet. (All of this came with its own set of challenges.)

Technology changes culture. And technology also changes business models.

Robert Iger, a former CEO of Disney, says it well:

"Technological advancements will eventually make older business models obsolete. You can either bemoan that and try with all your might to protect the status quo, or you can work hard to understand and embrace it with more enthusiasm and creativity than your competitors."

Robert Iger will remain known for making the decision to transform Disney's business model. In 2019, the company launched Disney+, a streaming service, which required Disney to pull out its content from other channels—meaning saying "no" to billions of euros in revenue from licensing content to TV channels and streaming platforms—in order to launch its new direct-to-consumer streaming service.

Disney realised that technology has been changing the culture. People are now expecting to watch their favourite movies and series on-demand. TV is in decline and streaming is growing. The company had to decide whether they were okay to destroy their old business model in order to be part of the new era of streaming. And they did it.

Technology influences demand

Technology can make people do new things by changing their environment.

The infrastructure of a city pushes its residents to behave in one way or another. The level of congestion, the access to reliable public transport, the ease of cycling around, and the walkability of a neighbourhood have a big impact on how people move around in a city—and on what they decide to do.

You're more likely to take the underground in New York, cycle in Amsterdam, and drive in Miami. It's all influenced by the infrastructure of these cities.

If a city installs new bike lanes, people will be more likely to decide to cycle around. For example, Seville created nearly 100 km of bike lanes in the 2000s. This led the number of cycling trips on a working day to increase from about 13,000 in 2005 to more than 70,000 in 2011.

New technology—like infrastructure—influences what people choose to do. It influences demand.

Leapfrogging

It's expensive to set up new infrastructure. Building highways or creating a landline network requires a lot of investment.

What may feel even more expensive is *to upgrade* the infrastructure. The upgraded system can improve the end-user experience, but doesn't necessarily lead to more revenue for the operator.

It's a question of cost vs. benefit.

If you rebuild the rail system between London and Paris to make Eurostar trains faster, it will cost a lot, but it's likely that passengers won't want to pay more. They're still getting from London to Paris. Saving 10 or 20 minutes doesn't make such a significant difference that it justifies raising the fares.

The need to balance cost and benefit gives an advantage to those who build a brand new infrastructure from scratch using the latest technology. They aren't held back by the fact that upgrading won't lead to more revenue or value being created. Leapfroggers can compress the time it took other players to get ahead of them.

This is why the Internet feels so much faster in Bucharest than in Paris. Bucharest built its network later and had access to better technology. Bucharest didn't have to upgrade old technology, while, in Paris, the benefit of a slightly faster Internet connection makes it harder to justify the cost of upgrading the infrastructure.

Most African countries didn't have to create local bank branches to get people to open bank accounts. Instead, they leapfrogged. Most people directly went from no bank to adopting digital banks through mobile phones. This is something that European banks are still working on.

Leapfrogging happens when an organisation or a business can progress rapidly through the adoption of modern systems without going through intermediary steps.

Zoom on Culture

Culture is inherently human. It's multifaceted and full of nuances. And it's always changing.

It's hard to faithfully capture and translate the zeitgeist into a set of insights. It requires an appreciation of group dynamics and human psychology, as well as a genuine understanding of humanity's past and today's social influences.

Not just "problems"

The reason I like to talk about culture or socio-cultural dynamics is that it elevates the way we look at new opportunities.

Entrepreneurs and companies often limit themselves to looking at opportunities through the lens of "problems". It's like saying: "Our customers have problem X, therefore there's an opportunity for us."

Yes, customer and user problems are a source of opportunities—but not the only one. Cool stuff, desires, and emotional aspirations also trigger opportunities. One could go through the exercise of reframing everything as "problems". But there are so many cases where it's too limiting.

Culture is broader than our problems. It's also about how we live, what we believe, and what we dream of. It's about our fears and our hopes. It's about how we interact with our community. It's about the expression of our personal identity.

It's one of the most important triggers of new opportunities. Culture has a massive influence on how we define what creates value for us, and therefore on the types of things we buy. It is particularly important in push sectors where there aren't many unmet needs and big customer problems to solve.

A fashion brand doesn't solve a "clothing problem". We're all well equipped. You may argue it solves a "confidence problem" or a need to feel part of a group. But again… this isn't enough to clearly define an opportunity in the fashion world. For this, you need a deeper understanding of the zeitgeist.

Also, it's not because you're the best at solving a problem that you'll be able to seize the opportunity.

WhatsApp has become the messaging app of choice. But it's not because it's the best solution to an "online communication problem" or the most secure. It's because it (luckily?) became part of the Western culture.

Connections and social norms

Social norms are informal rules that guide the way we connect to others.

I like how Seth Godin summarises the concept of culture in plain English: "People like us do things like this."

As humans, we aspire to belong to the groups we identify with.

We want to connect with people like us. We want to gain their respect. So we make the unconscious choice to live and think like them—doing everything that's needed to make us feel that we are part of those groups.

This is how culture becomes a foundation of our behaviours.

Culture gets things done

> *"How did Homo sapiens manage to [found] cities comprising tens of thousands of inhabitants and empires ruling hundreds of millions? The secret was probably the appearance of fiction. Large numbers of strangers can cooperate successfully by believing in common myths."*
>
> – YUVAL NOAH HARARI, Israeli Historian

Sharing the same worldview can enable people to get things done together. This is how we built cities, religions, and nations. Sharing a narrative can encourage a group of people to perform individual tasks that will support a common goal. Culture has the power to unlock large-scale human cooperation.

It even works when you don't know the people on the other side. This is how the Internet has been built. Let me share a couple of examples to illustrate:

1. In 2020, WordPress was used to power 39% of all websites in the world. This content management system was created as an open-source project in 2003. What's impressive is that most people who contribute to building the platform and the ecosystem around it have never met in person. But the WordPress culture and the common belief in democratising publishing on the open web are strong enough to get people to work and build things together.

2. For sharing the podcast episodes of GoudronBlanc, I use an open-source solution called Podlove. Just a few days after I started using it, I spotted a bug that was due to the iOS 14.5 update of Apple Podcast. I immediately connected with the Podlove community to explain the bug. Together—and even though we didn't know each other—we identified and solved the issue. They had created a warm and welcoming atmosphere that made me want to contribute. We were all connected through our passion for podcasting. And this culture enabled us to get things done as a group.

Today, the Internet culture is so vast that there's an insane amount of subcultures. Sometimes they replicate what's happening IRL (in real life), and sometimes they are unique to the medium.

Each of these subcultures also influences how things get done. The TikTok culture is different from the Instagram culture. It's not just the rules on the platforms that push the creation of different types of content, but also how people tacitly decide to behave together. If you have a question regarding your iPhone, it won't get answered in the same way on the MacRumors forum, on Apple Community, or on Stack Exchange. That's because each platform has a unique culture.

The long tail of cultures

A big mistake is to see culture as a set of values, beliefs, and references that *everyone* shares. The mistake is to call it *the* culture.

Even Star Wars, McDonald's, or Facebook aren't ubiquitous. Not everyone believes it's something that's for people like them.

There are multiple "cultures"—so many smaller groups who have their own beliefs and do things in their own way.

Here's a funny example: Try to get a dog lover to discuss pet preferences with a cat lover. Or even more specific, let the owner of a Yorkshire Terrier have a chat with someone who has a Golden Retriever. They will agree to disagree. But put two Yorkshire Terrier owners in the same room and they will share stories about the strong nature of these tiny little dogs.

There isn't such a thing as "mass culture". There's a wide range of *cultures*, a wide range of "people like us, do things like this".

Another example of a "long tail of culture" struck me when I stopped at a gas station in Belgium. On a sunny day, it is usual to see groups of people riding motorcycles in the countryside. Two groups of riders had parked their bikes in front of the shop. One group had racing style Japanese motorcycles. The other group had Harley Davidsons. Though everyone shared their passion for two-wheelers with loud engines, it was obvious that the two groups weren't part of the same subculture. They had no interest in interacting with one another. In their eyes, they felt they were too different from each other.

There's such a diversity of views and cultures. As you're looking for your next big opportunity, it's important to remind yourself that your company can't reach and please everyone. You must be able to say to a lot of people "this isn't for you".

Culture influences status

We define ourselves relative to the culture we're part of. It's not just about "me". "My identity" also depends on everyone else around "me".

Culture defines *what* is important; status defines *who* is important.

What's worth noting is that status in one culture isn't the same as status in another culture.

In the "investment banking culture", status is about money. Hosting a massive pool party, charting a jet, and being seen on a big yacht are ways to demonstrate high status. If you're the best at showing off and you can afford to do that repeatedly, you win the status game.

In the "zero waste culture", status is about how sustainable your lifestyle is. Avoid single-use plastic, composting, and buying second-hand clothes are seen as good things when you value sustainability above convenience.

These two examples are a simplification of reality. But you can imagine how the person who's used to bragging about charting a jet will struggle to be seen as cool among people who pride themselves on having stopped booking flights for the last few years.

Culture defines the rules of the status game. It tells us what's good and what's bad. And it influences what we aspire to and what we want to avoid.

Cultures overlap

There's a wide range of cultures. And so, each of us belongs to more than one culture. (It means that there must be such a thing as an eco-conscious investment banker.)

We all have a diversity of influences, interests, and groups we feel we belong to. Context tends to dial up or dial down certain areas of our lives.

Here's an example:

I love dancing salsa. One of the things I particularly like about salsa is how diverse the salsa community is. In London, salsa brings together people who may appear to have very little in common. Jobs go from lawyers to teachers to designers to software engineers to builders to accountants, etc. Some also run marathons, love knitting, or go to yoga classes. The age range is 18 to 80. And there are probably 10+ nationalities in the same room. There's an incredible diversity of interest. But all these people *together* form the salsa culture, which represents a market that creates big opportunities for event organisers, dancing schools, and salsa bands.

Depending on the context, we bring different versions of ourselves. Each of us is part of a number of cultures defined and shaped by our family background, friends, hobbies, job, and dreams and aspirations.

There's more than one culture. And cultures overlap.

A barrier to adoption

Culture is the biggest barrier to adopting new technology, new products, new brands.

If you want to sell something to a specific audience, your prospects must start believing that people like them do things like buying your proposition.

Try to get a 50-year-old person to use Snapchat or TikTok, or to wear a pair of Yeezy sneakers. They're likely to tell you: "This is not for me!", which means "I don't believe things like these are for people like me".

Many startups fail because their product or service didn't resonate with the zeitgeist. They may have been solving a problem—even a big problem. But they weren't able to become part of the culture.

CHAPTER SIX:

Diffusion of change

Change starts small and progressively spreads. But this progress isn't linear. If you want to anticipate how change might affect your business and create new opportunities, you need to understand the patterns of diffusion. It's all about timing. Let's use a wide-angle lens for that.

At the right time

You may have heard that "timing is everything". There isn't such a thing as the "right idea" if time isn't right for it.

If you're too early, you are not building on a strong enough business opportunity. It may cost you a lot until you can make material returns on your investments.

If you're too late, the market will be too mature, the competitors too big, and the opportunity far gone.

So, you want to get in on time, when the market is ready and the competitors are still not there yet. "Not too early, not too late" is the art of the game. And obviously, it's easier said than done because it's hard to anticipate how things will evolve.

Change rarely spreads in a linear way, which is what makes predicting the future a difficult endeavour. The good news is that when you observe change, it seems that it often follows similar patterns. Though you can't accurately predict change, you can rely on these patterns to prepare yourself for how change may spread over time.

Diffusion and adoption

In some cases, change happens to us. This is diffusion, i.e., the rate at which change spreads and impacts our lives. In some others, change spreads only when we adopt it. This is adoption, i.e., the rate at which *we* make change happen.

When diffusion happens, nobody asks for our opinion. No matter what, we have to accept what changed as a new fact in our lives. Be it an economic crisis, pollution, or a global pandemic, we have to embrace the change and how it affects us.

But in many cases, change is subject to adoption. It means that, for change to happen, someone must decide—consciously or unconsciously—to adopt it in order for change to spread. Here, *we* can decide to embrace change or not. Change depends on what we choose to do.

And sometimes, it's adoption that creates diffusion. For example, policies spread through adoption by lawmakers and public authorities. Then, the general public must embrace them as new facts of their lives—this is diffusion.

For example, the mayors of European capitals try to limit the number of cars in the cities and want to encourage the use of bicycles. From a macro perspective, we can see a gradual adoption of regulations that make it less attractive to drive a car in urban areas. This change first spreads through adoption by mayors and city councils, and then spreads through diffusion as it impacts city dwellers without them having much to say about it.

Diffusion (change happening to us) and adoption (us choosing to change) are two ways for change to spread. You'll see that in the following sections, I tend to use "diffusion" and "adoption" interchangeably, as both are about how change grows over time.

Visualising adoption

The process of adoption can be visualised as an S-curve. The "S" represents the cumulative adoption over time. As time passes, change reaches more people.

When you look at an S-curve, you notice three distinct phases of adoption:

1. It starts slowly – this is the *infancy phase*
2. It accelerates – this is the *growth phase*
3. It slows down – this is the *maturity phase*

Three phases of the S-curve

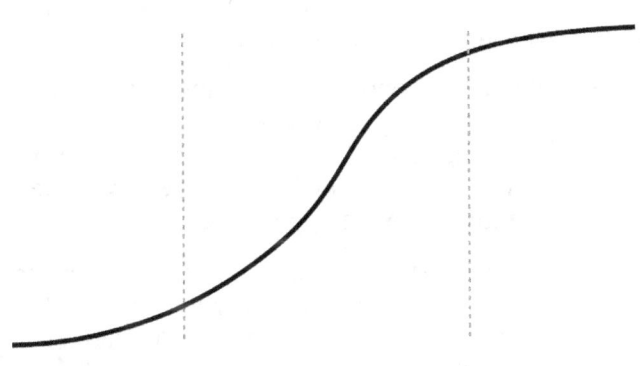

Infancy   Scaling   Maturity

This is how change spreads: It starts slowly, then it accelerates, then it slows down again.

Like on a dance floor

If you've ever been in a club too early, you have experienced how culture spreads within a group of people who don't know each other.

In the beginning, the dance floor is totally empty. No one dances. Then, someone decides to go first—most of the time finding bravery thanks to a few drinks. Some friends decide to join—often feeling quite uncertain about why they decided to go on the dance floor. Progressively, more and more people start dancing. When the number of people dancing increases, those who are at the bar feel more compelled to join the crowd. And at some point, dipping in and out of the dance floor just feels normal.

You may still see a few people who prefer to hang out at the bar. But overall, a new vibe has settled. It went from feeling awkward to go on the dance floor to totally normal.

Change happened.

Infancy vs. Maturity

A business doesn't grow in the same way at the infancy phase and maturity phase of an opportunity.

- When an opportunity is emerging, things are moving slowly. Everyone is wondering whether it's going to get big or remain niche. Businesses are in a discovery mode—unsure of whether they should pursue the opportunity.

- At the growth stage, demand accelerates. Companies who got in early focus on how to scale in order to serve the growing market as fast as possible. There's still lots of room for growth and other players are looking at the space wondering how they could also get in.

- Once the opportunity has reached maturity, growth becomes a zero-sum game. To grow, you must either steal market share from the competition or acquire competitors.

Here's an example about the Internet:

At the beginning of the 1990s, the Internet was like the Wild West. The World Wide Web made instant global connectivity possible. But this was just the theory. In practice, it was hard to see whether it was something just for the nerds or something that could become mainstream.

This was the infancy.

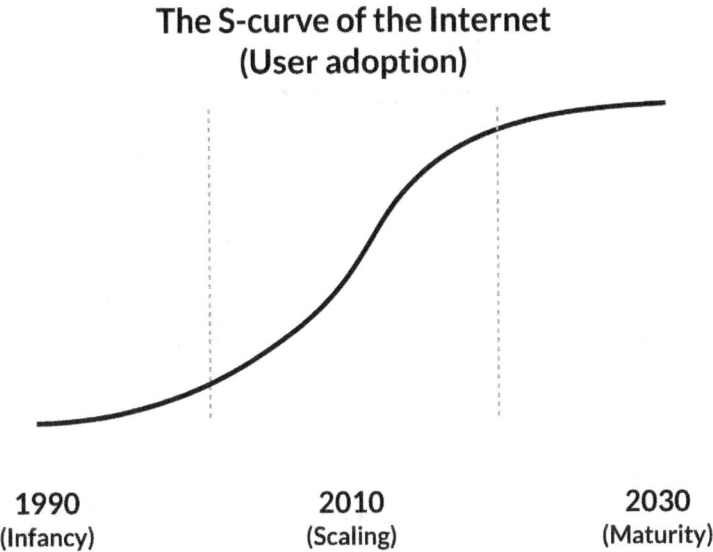

The S-curve of the Internet (User adoption)

1990
(Infancy)

2010
(Scaling)

2030
(Maturity)

Then, tech companies started proving that the Internet could help address many human needs by revolutionising the way we access music and video, connect to one another, do our shopping, or even meet our partner.

Internet businesses were facilitating the transition from older technology (e.g., pen and paper, CDs, and brick and mortar) to the digital world. And there was a lot of stuff to do.

This was the growth phase.

But now, things are slowing down. Internet businesses are competing less with pen and paper, and more with other internet businesses. The opportunity to digitise the brick-and-mortar world has reached maturity. This is the third phase of the S-curve. It means that, in many cases, businesses are now in a near zero-sum game world. If you want new customers, you need to steal them from your direct competitors—no longer from pen and paper.

So now, everyone is after the next S-curve.

Will it be machine learning, blockchain, augmented

reality, virtual reality, or a combination of all of them at the same time?

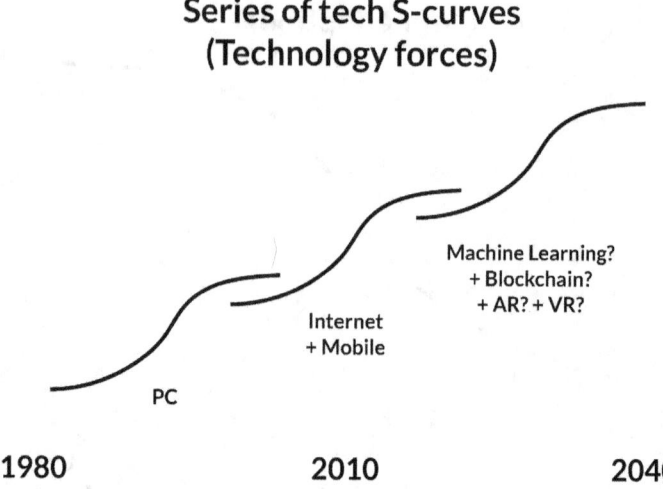

Series of tech S-curves (Technology forces)

- PC
- Internet + Mobile
- Machine Learning? + Blockchain? + AR? + VR?

1980 — 2010 — 2040

New technology has transformed every sector—but some more than others. Since 1990, retail, media, and banking have been particularly impacted.

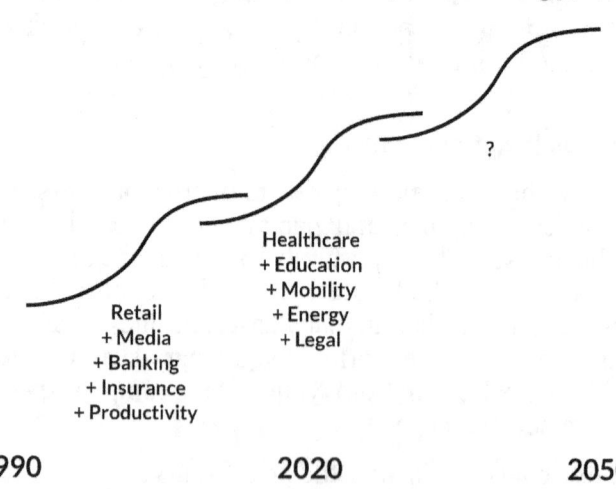

Series of S-curves (Sectors transformed by technology)

- Retail + Media + Banking + Insurance + Productivity
- Healthcare + Education + Mobility + Energy + Legal
- ?

1990 — 2020 — 2050

Now, it seems that startup investors are looking more at healthcare, education, mobility, and the legal sector. But then, what's next?

Crazy!?

> *"All truth passes through three stages. First, it is ridiculed. Second, it is violently opposed. Third, it is accepted as being self-evident."*
>
> – ARTHUR SCHOPENHAUER, Philosopher

When we're at the beginning of an adoption curve, change often feels like a crazy thing is happening.

Wearing a mask everywhere felt awkward for people in the Western world when it became compulsory in most countries in 2020. By the end of 2020, it nearly felt normal.

In the early 1990s, the Internet was only for the nerds. It was obscure to most people. The same seems to be happening now with blockchain technology. You may wonder: "Who are these people who are getting excited about 'decentralised apps', 'non-fungible digital assets', and 'smart contracts'?"

In the 1950s, few people would have felt ok wearing a T-shirt without a shirt on top. T-shirts were seen as underwear. Now it's a given that anyone can feel confident wearing a T-shirt without any on top.

In 2010, you may not have been taken seriously if you were working from home five days a week. In 2020, everyone can get their head around it.

In the 1970s, people who worried about the environmental impact of consumer goods were called hippies. In 2020, people who don't worry about this are seen as deniers.

So what's the crazy stuff happening today that could become the new normal tomorrow?

The hype cycle

Often, our perception of the adoption process gets distorted. It's the buzzword effect. Everyone talks about it. But not much is happening. There's more hype than impact.

It's as if everyone was hallucinating collectively. You still get some naysayers. But there's a general sense of enthusiasm for the potential of a particular technology—without much concrete evidence that it works. The buzz thrives on social media and on PowerPoint slides. Yet, the impact is nowhere to be seen.

Gartner, a research company, calls this the "hype cycle". It highlights the distorted view of the craze versus what is happening in reality.

According to their model, nascent technology gets more publicity than it deserves. The excitement comes from the massive potential that covers the lack of working use cases.

It can take a while before people realise that the enthusiasm didn't match the reality. At this stage, we're at a crossroad. Either someone finds a compelling use case for the new technology and it gets adopted, or it just goes nowhere and people discard it.

The five phases of the hype cycle

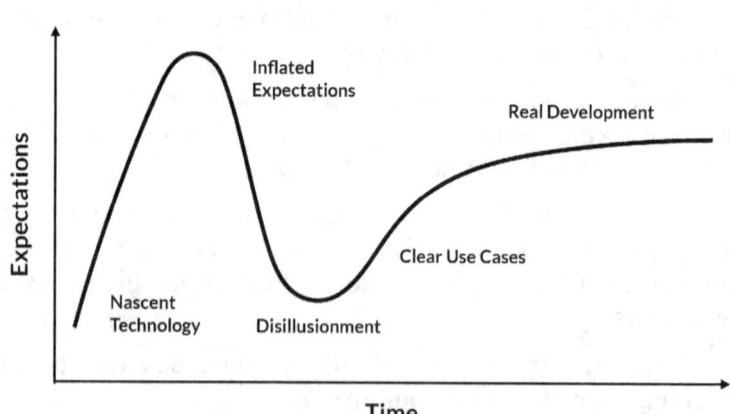

The hype cycle model can also be applied to culture, some areas of economics, and new policies and regulations.

The tipping point

When you look at an S-curve, you see a moment where it goes from flat to steep. The tipping point is this blurred moment where change goes from unnoticed to obvious. Change has reached a critical mass, momentum starts to build, and adoption accelerates.

This could almost feel like an overnight event. But in reality, this is the result of an infancy phase that may have taken months, years, or sometimes decades.

The questions are: *When is change going to reach the tipping point?* And, above all, *will reaching the tipping point ever happen?*

You may have heard the phrase "crossing the chasm".

A cultural trend, a technology, or a new type of policy that doesn't succeed to cross the chasm will die or remain small. Adoption didn't reach the tipping point. The curve just stays flat.

The tipping point

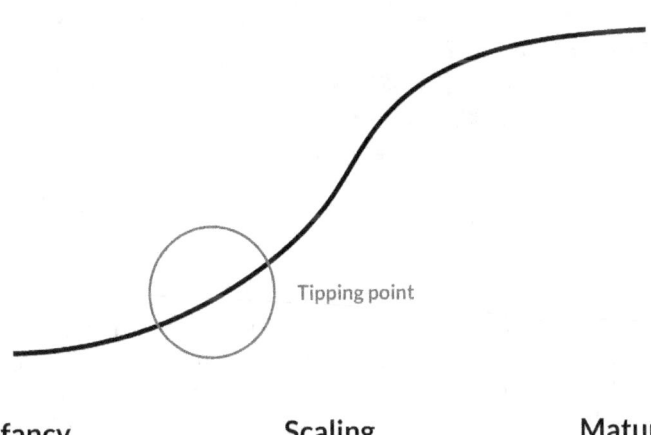

Infancy   Scaling   Maturity

If adoption crosses the chasm, then you may observe a rapid uptake. This is the steep part of the S-curve.

Exponential trajectory

There's a moment in the S-curve where you see that the curve gets very steep. It almost looks like the curve of an exponential function.

At this stage, diffusion or adoption accelerates.

Some S-curves get closer to "exponential growth" than others. And it seems that recently the way change spreads has accelerated in the last few decades.

We can observe this in the way cheaper hardware and new apps have been adopted. It took more than 50 years for the telephone to reach 50 million users. PC did it in 14 years. Mobile phones achieved this in about 12 years. It took Facebook four years to get 50 million users. And WeChat did it in a year.

Time to 50 million users

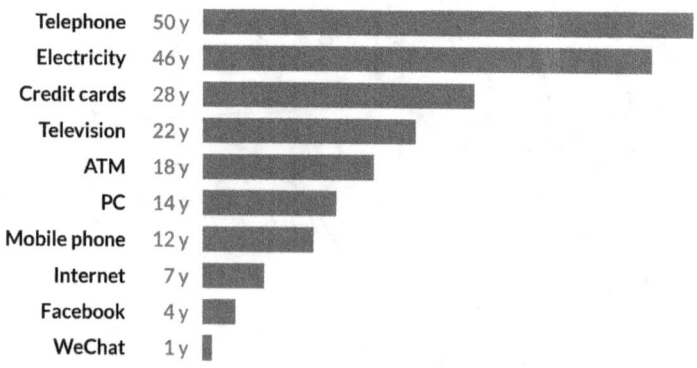

Of course, it's easier and cheaper to install an app on your phone than to build a landline. But, I'm sure you'll agree that the immediate connection to the rest of the world that the Internet created also plays a big role in accelerating the pace of diffusion.

It's not just technology that can spread faster. Culture, policies, environment, and economical change all move faster in a more connected world.

Here are a couple of questions to keep in mind when you observe change:

1. How fast is it going to spread?
2. Is there anything that is likely to accelerate how change will spread in the future?

New paradigm

A story has a beginning, a middle, and an end.

This is the same for the S-curve of diffusion. It starts at the infancy phase where change is hidden. Then, there's a period of acceleration. During this transition phase, we reach a tipping point where change becomes obvious to most. That's it! A new paradigm is established. After that, diffusion slows down, as it reaches the laggards.

There's a world before the shift. There's a world after the shift.

Two simple questions can start your journey into figuring out these new paradigms: "What's true today that wasn't true before?" and "What will be true tomorrow that isn't true yet?"

CHAPTER SEVEN:

Foresight

If you want to make sure you're building a business that has longevity, you need to have a point of a view on how the future could play out. It will allow you to be aware of the forces of change that will impact your business model in the future.

For this, you must go through a hypothetical "business time travel". So, let's put on some future-proofing lenses.

Arbitrage vs. Investment

Short-term opportunities can be profitable. These types of arbitrage can bring significant revenue to companies that know how to spot them and react quickly. Pursuing arbitrage opportunities is likely to be already part of what your company does. It's very much "business as usual".

- It's the chocolate brand launching a new matcha flavour that builds on the trend for green tea matcha.

- It's a restaurant adding vegetarian options on its menu, because the owner understands it can serve a wider range of customers that way.

- It's the agency that accepts a contract beyond its in-house capabilities and hires freelancers to deliver the project.
- It's the publishing company that releases a new edition of a best-selling book for its 10th anniversary.
- It's the film production studio that makes the sequel of a successful movie to leverage a past box office hit.
- It's the retailer that makes special offers for Black Friday.

It's all incremental. Arbitrage is an add-on to your value proposition. It helps maximise the revenue of an existing business model. But it's unlikely to lead to the next big thing for your company.

Here, I want to focus on "big opportunities". Those opportunities require some investment, and should possibly lead to some great upside. It doesn't always mean lots of capital expenditure. But it will require a minimum of time, skills, and energy to go after them.

When you consider possible opportunities, you want to pick the ones that will allow your company to capture material value. To be worth the effort, the opportunity must have longevity. And this requires you to consider what might happen in the future.

Foresight thinking vs. Design thinking

> *"Design thinking is a human-centred approach to innovation that draws from the designer's toolkit to integrate the needs of people, the possibilities of technology, and the requirements for business success."*
>
> – TIM BROWN, Executive Chair, IDEO

Design thinking is a popular innovation process. It is known for being "human-centred" and "iterative". The methodology emphasises the importance of empathy and putting the customer and the user at the centre. It also embraces an iterative "test and learn" approach that encourages testing your assumptions in the real world—and doing so continuously.

As a process, design thinking is a proven way to generate solutions to current customer problems. It especially helps to spot today's opportunities.

Foresight thinking complements and pushes design thinking a step beyond. It focuses on a longer period. It's a disciplined methodology that explores what could happen in the future. In sports lingo, it's about trying to anticipate where the ball will bounce next.

Here's a definition shared by the OECD:

> *"Foresight uses a range of methodologies, such as scanning the horizon for emerging changes, analysing megatrends and developing multiple scenarios, to reveal and discuss useful ideas about the future."*

Foresight doesn't attempt to offer a definitive view of the future. By definition, there's no fact about the future. You can't get the future right. But expanding your view beyond what's happening now will help you understand the market and industry dynamics in the long term.

Foresight thinking relies on a deep understanding of human psychology and socio-cultural dynamics. But it also looks at the other areas of the STEER framework such as how technological, economic, environmental, and regulatory changes could shape tomorrow and create new opportunities.

Combining design thinking and foresight thinking gives you a frame that allows you to be aware of potential threats, spot long-lasting opportunities, and be clear on what the associated risks are.

Forming your thesis

> *"Thesis driven investing involves drawing a picture of where your particular area of focus is going. I like to take a five- to ten-year view. And once you have mapped out that picture, it becomes your thesis. And you evaluate every investment you make in the context of that thesis."*
>
> – FRED WILSON, Partner, Union Square Ventures

Your thesis is the output of your foresight work. It's an informed view of the future that you rely on to discover, assess, and choose potential opportunities, while helping you avoid the noise and the fads.

Conventionally, futures research tends to show up as a lengthy process because it has been codified by academics and large organisations to inform public policies and corporate strategy. Though it emerged from strategic planning, it's been recently adapted to be better suited for the needs of startups and venture capital investment.

Here, I want to use foresight with a more practical innovation-oriented approach. My aim isn't to present a detailed research process, but to share down-to-earth considerations that will allow you to form your thesis. This thesis will serve as an additional lens to spot future lasting opportunities for your company and help you evaluate the associated risks.

In this chapter, I'd like to give you some advice on how to define the scope of your foresight research, collect data and information about the future, organise what you observed and learnt, and get your company to align on a shared thesis.

The way I present foresight in this chapter feels linear. That's because it's the easiest way to explain it in a book. However, in practice, the process isn't that sequential. You may have to iterate more than once, moving back and forth between two phases as you uncover new insight.

Defining

As for any research, your first step must be to define the scope of your work. Defining is about making sure you have enough focus so you aren't burning too many resources (time, money, energy) in your exploration of the future.

The objective here is to create a view of the future that can be used to spot and test your next big opportunities. It's not a crystal-balling exercise. There's no point trying to predict the future since it can't be predicted. But it's about having thought through what could happen to make sure you're not putting your eggs in a basket that is about to vanish.

In this section, I'll share elements that will help you define your foresight exploration, so you can be reassured that you're focusing on what will be useful for you to spot opportunities.

Constraints mean focus

"Style is the outcome of constraint."

– ANDRÉ MAUROIS, French Author

Exploring the future can feel daunting; there's just so much you can cover and get to think about. If you have no constraint, you will find it hard to progress and reach any tangible learning about the future.

You want to avoid "boiling the ocean". You won't have the resources to carry a thorough exploration of the future. So you need to clearly define the scope of your foresight research.

Having limited resources here is an advantage. It forces you to be practical, to focus your energy on the right topics, and to quickly get to something useful for spotting opportunities.

Even large companies don't have the luxury to buy

lengthy studies of the future. And in any case, the senior leadership will be more interested in hearing about the big opportunities for their company—the next step after your foresight research—rather than in the study of the future itself. They will want to understand the "so what", i.e., "so now that we know all this, what do we do as a company?" they would ask.

Research funnel

As I explained, your foresight research should have a clear focus. But this scope shouldn't be set in stone. It will evolve over time. You can think of this as a funnel: It starts broad and narrows as you progress.

At the beginning of your research, you want to be open to any possibility, so you allow yourself to explore related industries and look at what's happening in other countries. You have permission to immerse yourself by adopting a 360° view to get a sense of what life could feel like in the future.

But quickly, you will have to narrow your scope. You will notice that you start gravitating around topics that are closer to the sectors that your business could be involved in. These are the areas where you'll do more in-depth research.

Starting broad pushes you to go beyond your preconception. The point of exploring the future is to stretch your thinking and imagine more than a linear progression of what's happening today. It's about finding forces of change that will distort that linear path and create a future that we may not be envisioning right now. But you also want to remain practical and get to a position that will allow you to spot new opportunities.

While it's important to think expansively, it's equally important to know where to narrow down your focus so you can reach a tangible outcome.

From *your* perspective

The focus of your foresight research depends on your company and its current and long-term needs. A large corporate won't look at the future in the same way as a starting entrepreneur will. They have different stakes in play.

You'll need to set a timeframe and geographic focus. This will depend on your company's priorities and your sector. An industrial group will need to have a look at what will happen over the next 10-20 years because it has to manage capital-intensive projects, which could have a payback period of several decades.

An early-stage investor will have a shorter timeframe. They will usually look at the next 5-10 years, as it is roughly the time they will hold an investment in a startup. Early-stage investors have to sense-check the opportunities they spot to make sure they will still be good opportunities for public investors in case of an initial public offering or for a company that would acquire that startup within the following 8-10 years.

A startup founder will follow the same timeframe as their potential investors. Their ability to show that they are working on a business opportunity that will be increasingly important in the coming years is essential.

In general, I would recommend setting a timeframe of 5-10 years. It depends on the sectors, but it becomes hard to make any prediction beyond 10 years. In terms of geographic constraints, the most common is to look at the national level. But again, it may or may not be suitable for your company. Use this rule of thumbs as a starter and decide what makes the most sense for you.

Clarity on the "why"

Defining the focus of your foresight research requires you to be clear on why you want to have a view on what could happen in the future.

From a general standpoint, there are two reasons:

1. You want to use your thesis on the future to help you spot your next business opportunities;
2. You already have a sense of where the opportunities are and you want to explore what could happen in the future to help you check that you're going after the right opportunity.

Then, there are more specific reasons that depend on your company's context.

For an entrepreneur who wants to create a new venture, it's all about figuring out what to work on. "Well, I want to find an opportunity for my new business."

A venture capital firm needs a thesis for two reasons. On one hand, it needs a compelling view of the future to secure money from their limited partners, i.e., the companies that invest in venture capital funds. On the other hand, it needs a rationale that will guide the scouting and decision-making process for its future investments. A thesis helps achieve these two priorities.

A large corporate will need a thesis to decide what to do next. It could be that the company is at the crossroad of reconsidering its strategy. The landscape is changing and the leadership is afraid that the company's current value propositions won't be relevant in the future. The foresight research will help anticipate what could happen and decide what's the best course for action for the coming years. A thesis can also demonstrate industry leadership to shareholders and motivate employees by showing what will be possible in the future.

Who

In your research, you will have to involve various stakeholders. These are the people (internal or external) who have an interest and stake in the issues you will be exploring.

Internal stakeholders

Internal stakeholders include employees, colleagues, team members, management, board members, and investors. Your internal stakeholders can bring a wealth of experience and a view on what could happen in the future, as well as what it can mean for your company's resources and core capabilities.

It's important to engage with internal stakeholders at different levels to make sure that you know where your company stands. This will be key when you'll have to choose a thesis and make sure your company is aligned with it. If you are part of the leadership team, you will benefit from challenging your beliefs by talking to your people, as well as your shareholders.

Be mindful that internal stakeholders tend to have narrow views of the future. As I mentioned before, the more experience someone has the more difficult it is to challenge their own beliefs. You want to rely on their expertise, but balance this with the beginner's mindset. Choose the people who have an interesting point of view on the matter and make sure you bring a diversity of opinions.

External stakeholders

External stakeholders are customers, the customers of your customers, partners, suppliers, competitors, government, researchers, and experts. They will be bringing an outside perspective of the future.

Talking to external stakeholders is a great way to broaden your thinking and test your assumptions about what the future could look like.

Note that it sometimes happens that all the people working in a sector are guilty of industry-wide groupthink. It's often the case when the future seems to push in the direction that may wipe out their current business model. I'm thinking of the music sector in the 2000s. It seems that many players buried their heads in the sand and overlooked the move from CDs to MP3. In that case, you will hugely benefit from nurturing the views from outsiders, i.e., new entrants or people who work in other sectors.

Customers can be a great source of insight. But it tends to be challenging to get them to project themselves in the future. It's good practice to discuss with early adopters. They will help you spot emerging trends and new behaviours. But at this stage, use what you learn from them more as inspiration than concrete insight.

Scanning

When you scan the horizon, you look far away, carefully trying to get some information about what's in front of you.

This is the same process when you want to understand what could happen in the future. Scanning is the step where you're gathering information. You're collecting data points that help create a picture of what the future could look like.

The key here is to distinguish the different types of data and information you can collect. Let me explain.

Constant vs. Change

The first important distinction to make is between *constant* and *change*, i.e., what's likely to remain the same and what's likely to change.

Some things are constant. For example, Maslow's pyramid of needs will likely continue to be an accurate description of people's priorities in life. We need to eat and need to feel safe. And when we feel confident these needs are fulfilled, we move to another level of the pyramid. It'll remain the same.

And some other things change. Over the last two decades, we've seen the continuous growth of e-commerce. In 2021, it reached 15-30% of addressable retail in Europe. It will likely keep growing. The people who got used to the convenience of ordering online won't suddenly shift back to buying everything offline. And more online services will make it even easier and more compelling to order on the Internet.

Whether things will change also depends on your timeframe. If you're looking at the next 3-5 years, you can assume that the level of urbanisation won't significantly change. In the next 10-15 years, it's possible to see an urban exodus. Indeed, change that requires big commitments from a person or a business will take longer to spread. Moving to a new location isn't as easy as deciding to buy something online instead of going to a shop.

Once you've identified *what* will change, you need to figure *how* it will change. As I noted in the previous chapter, there are several types of change. There's linear change, exponential change, radical change, yo-yo type of change (swinging back and forth), etc.

Uncertainties

> *"There are known knowns; there are things we know we know. We also know there are known unknowns; that is to say, we know there are some things we do not know. But there are also unknown unknowns—the ones we don't know we don't know."*
>
> – DONALD RUMSFELD,
> Former Secretary of Defense, United States

Among the things that will change, there's *change you can foresee* and there's *change that's harder to predict*. The challenge is to separate what you can be confident about from the things that are uncertain.

It's important to be clear on what you can't predict. First, it allows you to stay true to what you can anticipate. Second, you can make sure you monitor how uncertainties change over time.

There are uncertainties across the five forces of change. A major technological unlock can be counted as uncertainty. Will augmented reality become widely used? Uncertainties can also be questions about economics or politics. What will the price of crude oil be in 2025? How much will the pound sterling or Bitcoin be worth in 2022? Will the United States elect a Democrat or a Republican president in 2024?

Uncertainty gradually reduces as we reach some key milestones. In the early 1990s, it was incredibly difficult to predict what the Internet would allow us to achieve. But later in the 2000s, once the Internet started to spread massively, it was easier to create a picture about the future of online commerce.

Today, we are facing other technological uncertainties. For example, we know that self-driving cars are in the making. In 2021, there are already many companies piloting their technology. What's uncertain is when we'll see autonomous vehicles becoming a valid option to travel, and also what impact it will have on how we travel, how we live, and how we shop.

So what do you do when there's something that you can't predict? A solution is to create what-if scenarios. *"What happens if [an uncertain event] happens?"* You'll find more on that later, in the next section.

Wild cards

There's a distinction to make between the *expected* and the *unexpected*. While some uncertainties can be expected, there are things that you just can't expect. These are total blind spots.

Who will be the president of France in 2027 is hard to predict. But you can expect that change will happen. Meanwhile, the sanitary crisis triggered by the spread of COVID-19 in 2020 was totally unexpected. You just couldn't know.

This is a wild card, or what Nicholas Nassim Taleb calls a "black swan" event. It's a major-effect event that is so unlikely to happen that it comes as a surprise.

Most wild card events are so improbable that it's

extremely hard to even acknowledge that they could happen. Who would have foreseen the unprecedented scale of the impact that COVID-19 had on the world? Who knows when the next major economic crisis will happen?

It's important to be aware that wild card events could happen. It allows you to make the distinction between wild cards and uncertainties. But you just can't base your future strategy on what can't be expected.

What's interesting to note is that wild cards are often rationalised after the fact. In hindsight, things always make much more sense. And there's always someone who will claim that they had predicted the wild card event was about to happen. There's always "a guy who had predicted the 2008 crisis". Prophets...

Trends

Trends reflect a pre-existing diffusion of change. A trend indicates the general direction of what has been changing.

You notice trends by looking at past events and infer how change will continue to happen. To help you spot major trends, you can rely on the STEER lenses.

A few examples of trends:

- The growing role of machine learning and artificial intelligence;
- The demand for more sustainable and eco-friendly products;
- The emerging interest in digital detox, i.e., reconnecting to "real" life by staying away from electronic devices.

Identifying a trend is the result of extrapolation. You've observed a specific pattern of change and you extrapolate how this will spread in the future. Trends are the assumption that change will continue in the same direction.

You may have noticed that more and more recent

graduates are okay to choose a lower paid job if it gives them a better work-life balance and allows them to work on something that they consider to be more meaningful. This new attitude towards work is the pattern of change. You could extrapolate from it that there's an increasing desire for making a positive impact in the world by doing meaningful work. It's a trend that every employer must pay attention to.

Trends vs. Fads

> *"A fad is a short-term phenomenon that might be profitable, but a fad doesn't last long enough to do a company much good."*
>
> – AL RIES, Marketing Consultant

Trends differ from fads in their longevity. While trends are the gradual and lasting diffusion of change, fads result from the interpretation people make of a specific change, resulting in its sudden—but short-lived—importance.

Al Ries and Jack Trout gave a lovely poetic explanation of fads in *The 22 Laws of Marketing*:

> *"A fad is a wave in the ocean, and a trend is the tide. A fad gets a lot of hype, and a trend gets very little. Like a wave, a fad is very visible, but it goes up and down in a big hurry. Like the tide, a trend is almost invisible, but it's very powerful over the long term."*

Trends are the expression of changes that are happening. Fads are just the hype about something that won't last.

The mistake you want to avoid is to gear up for a fad as if it was a trend. There's little benefit in investing in an opportunity that will disappear as fast as it appeared. So here is the question: *"Is it a trend or is it just a fad?"*

Is crypto technology a trend or a fad? Is augmented reality a trend or a fad? Is remote working a trend or a fad? Are electric cars a trend or a fad? Are plant-based alternatives to meat a trend or a fad?

Signals

> *"The future is already here, it's just not very evenly distributed."*
>
> – WILLIAM GIBSON, Essayist

Signals of change are things you see that indicate that change could be underway. They help you spot emerging trends. When there's no pre-existing pattern of change, no trends, you try to look for signals. Scanning for signals is about noticing small events that could be predictors of change.

A signal can be a new product, a newly adopted policy, a marketing decision, or emerging consumer behaviour. It's something that catches your attention as being an indication that something bigger could happen. Signals are a small or local change that has the potential to grow in scale.

Signals are both the evidence of change and the inspiration to imagine how things could be in the future. *"I saw that [signal] which could mean that in the future... [implications for tomorrow]."*

In the 1970s, you could have said: "I saw that Patagonia published a catalogue in 1972 advocating for 'clean climbing' asking its customers to be mindful of nature and its limited resources." It's your *signal*. This could mean that in the future: "Consumers will demand that their favourite brands act more responsibly and make products and services that are more sustainable." These are possible *implications for tomorrow*.

I took an example from the past for illustrative purposes. It is obviously simpler to notice signals in the past, as they become the data points that form a trend.

Noticing signals

> *"Learning about the future is learning about change."*

– FREIJA VAN DUIJNE and PETER BISHOP, Futurologists

Signals are the indicators of emergent phenomena. To notice signals, you could look at early adopters, i.e., people, locations, and organisations that are known to embrace novelty and be at the forefront of what will be possible in the future.

The Nordic countries are often seen as trendsetters in public policy. San Francisco tends to be in the vanguard of tech developments. Paris, New York, London, and Milan have been known to set the tone in terms of fashion.

You could also look at people and organisations who are willing to take risks. For example, you could assume that many of Elon Musk's endeavours are signals of what will captivate people's interest in the future: renewable energy, electric vehicles, colonising Mars, creating faster long-distance transport, or building a bridge between technology and our mind.

Signals vs. Noise

> *"Distinguishing the signal from the noise requires both scientific knowledge and self-knowledge: the serenity to accept the things we cannot predict, the courage to predict the things we can, and the wisdom to know the difference."*
>
> – NATE SILVER, American Statistician

When you're trying to notice new signals, you also encounter a lot of noise. It's important (and not easy) to distinguish signals from the ambient noise. Is what you've noticed a signal? Or is it just noise?

A signal should help you imagine the future. It's a data point that has some sort of predictive value—either because of the origin of the data or because it is part of a pattern that tells you something about the future.

Signals indicate that there's some change happening.

Noise distracts you from your research. It has no predictive value, and therefore is pointless. Or it gives some information, but that isn't relevant for what you're trying to understand about the future.

It often requires putting a few related signals together to see a pattern forming in front of you before you're able to say whether the signals are relevant and important.

So you must make sure that you're looking for predictive and relevant data points. It can help to have hypotheses.

Hypotheses

A hypothesis is an attempt at conceptualising what is happening in the world. At the scanning stage, it can be helpful to use hypotheses, as they will create a structure to guide your research.

There are two ways to go about coming up with hypotheses: deduction and induction. Let me explain how each works.

The deductive process is top-down. It means that you start with a hypothesis (general view of the world) and you support it with your observations (specific signals).

The inductive process is bottom-up. You begin here by observing things (specific signals), trying to group them into cohesive patterns (general view of the world). These become the hypotheses that you will then continue to test by finding additional signals.

Now, I'd like to bring this to life with a couple of examples.

Deduction

Because of the rise of concerns about the impact of our society on the environment, we can assume that sustainability will be a major trend that will shape what people decide to buy and allow companies to create new sources of value. This is a hypothesis.

To reinforce my confidence in that hypothesis, I can, for example, look at the startup landscape in the consumer goods sector. It's striking that many new flourishing companies appear to be sustainably native brands. They put sustainability at the centre of their value propositions and the way they operate. They do not only sell a product, they also sell a positive social or environmental commitment. And this is what seems to make them so interesting in the eyes of their audiences.

Here, we have a deduction, i.e., a general hypothesis that we tested with signals we can see in the world.

Induction

Without knowing much about blockchain technology, you can't ignore the frequent mentions of cryptocurrencies, NFTs (non-fongible tokens), DAOs (decentralised autonomous organisations), and smart contracts. It's like what happened with .com companies in the 90s. There may be too much hype about crypto, but the momentum we observe clearly demonstrates a large interest in the area and a trend towards the use of more decentralised technologies. If this view of the world is right, it could trigger some potential long-lasting opportunities.

Here, we have an induction, i.e., a set of signals we observed that lead us to a hypothesis on how all these things relate to each other.

Deductions and inductions are the two ways we use to organise our thinking. It's helpful to have them in mind when you want to come up with the hypotheses that will structure your research.

Drivers vs. Blockers

As I noted earlier, it is hard to predict the pace of change. But it can help to identify the factors that are driving change and those that may slow it down.

Drivers are all the factors that accelerate change. These

driving factors could be anything from the hype in the media to a recent technological breakthrough to massive investments in an area or subsidies from the government.

Blockers are factors that tend to mitigate the change that is happening, e.g., a conservative cultural heritage, R&D limitations, and strict regulations.

Here's an example: While digitalisation has spread across most industries, the legal sector seems to be lagging behind. That's because there are many blockers in this industry. Culturally, lawyers are reluctant to change. In general, they don't like adopting new technology. There are also inherent blockers, as justice is less black and white than the numbers that drive Wall Street.

Even after you've aligned on a thesis, it remains important to monitor the drivers and blockers. You want to carry on having visibility on the factors that may accelerate or hinder change, and therefore impact your business model.

Doing research

There are many ways you can scan for trends and signals. Here are a few options:

- Firsthand observations: Look at what's happening around you. Look at what your potential customers are doing. Observe.

- Desk research: Search online for trends. Read forums. Go on social media. Look at what influencers say and do.

- Testing new technology: Use new stuff. Try the latest gadgets. Buy some Bitcoin. Experiment with what's not mainstream yet.

- Customer interviews: Invite customers to talk about their challenges, their aspirations, and their frustrations.

- Quant study: Run surveys. Ask groups of people about what they like, what their problems are, what they've tried, and what they believe in.

- Talking to experts: Hang out with people who are fully immersed in the new technologies, and new policies. Get to talk to people who are at the edge of the cultural zeitgeist.

- Competitive analysis: Look at what your boldest and most ambitious competitors are doing.

- Looking at proxies from another sector: Go beyond your industry. How do companies in other sectors approach things? What does it tell you about what could happen in your industry?

The opportunity mindset I mentioned in chapter 2 is at the core of scanning. You need to be inquisitive by being curious, trying to spot patterns, and experimenting as much as possible.

The best way to learn about the future is to immerse yourself in the new.

Organising

In this phase, you will make sense of the data you collected and organise your thinking in a way that will be actionable.

Once you have identified upcoming trends and early signals, you want to bring your observations together so that you can create a view of the future business environment. It's about painting the scene of what could happen in the future to help you spot new opportunities and make decisions regarding which ones you want to go after.

Future landscape

> *"The future has many names: For the weak, it means the unattainable. For the fearful, it means*

the unknown. For the courageous, it means opportunity."

– VICTOR HUGO, French Author

It's one thing to spot trends. It's another to make it real by articulating them into a coherent representation of how things could be in the future. For this, you need to create a view of the future landscape: a view of the *market* (your prospects and customers) and a view of the *industry* (your potential competitors, partners, and suppliers).

What will the market look like? In what context will your customers live in the future? What will they be doing? What will be their goals, desires, and needs? What will be getting in the way of achieving what they want? What will frustrate them?

What will the industry look like? Who will be the main players? What will their business model be? What will the value chain look like? How will various players work with one another? What will the competition look like? What will be the state of technology? What regulations will be in place?

This future landscape will be a fertile ground for spotting big opportunities

A well-constructed view of the future landscape must contain enough detail to be useful for understanding the market and the industry in the future. But not so much as to become overly specific and irrelevant to the issues of interest.

Depending on what you're uncovering, there are various ways to organise your thinking and bring the future landscape to life. I'll share some inspiration in the following sections.

Conjecturing

Conjecturing is the beginning of your journey in organising your thoughts. But it's likely to already start while you're scanning.

A conjecture is a supposition about something based on incomplete information. You don't have a lot of evidence, but you sense something is going on.

It's not a final say on anything. It's more of a first step. It allows you to start organising your observations, while keeping things open and not drawing any final conclusion.

To capture your conjectures, you can use the following format: *"There's something about…"*. What follows is your supposition, i.e., what your instinct is telling you based on early scanning.

If you're exploring the future of food, and you have observed a few trends and signals. You would probably find yourself saying: "There's something about people wanting to go back to a more sustainable way of living by eating local, organic, and healthier food." This conjecture could become one of the threads that will help you organise your research.

It's all about decoding signals and trends. *"If [signal A] and [signal B] are happening, what does it mean?"* Conjecturing is a starter in exploring the "so what" of your observations.

Theming

The organising process can be quite daunting. There is a lot to absorb. For me, a great way to organise my thinking is to identify key themes.

Once you've gathered a fair amount of data and insight, you can start grouping your observations into themes. Doing so should help you see some patterns emerging. This is very much of a bottom-up exercise. You start from single elements and ladder them up into themes.

In 2020 and 2021, we've seen a few odd events on the

financial market. For example, there were individuals buying shares of Hertz even though the company was filing for bankruptcy. You may also have heard of the January 2021 bubble around GameStop, a video game retailer. Despite GameStop not being in great shape, the stock gained popularity on the Internet, which made it reach nearly 30 times its value in less than a few days. Dogecoin is a cryptocurrency that was invented as a parody of Bitcoin based on the Shiba Inu breed of dog (Yes, for real!). In May 2021, the market capitalisation reached €85 billion from a high of €310 million a year earlier. (Note that €85 billion is bigger than 80% of the companies in the S&P 500).

There's a theme emerging here. Bloomberg's Matt Levin talks about the "boredom markets hypothesis", which he defines as people investing when buying stocks and other asset classes is more fun than other things they could be doing for fun.

At first, your themes will be conjectures. As you get more and more evidence, you may tweak some themes, create new ones, and maybe get rid of some others.

Shifts

Shifts are a change in state. An easy way to think about it is that the world goes *"from [past or current state] to [future state]"*.

You can use shifts to capture and emphasise what is changing and how.

For example, as I noted before, we're seeing a big shift from people willing to work for money to people willing to work for meaning. Younger generations tend to choose their jobs depending on the impact they feel they will have and the meaning it has for them. In the past, it was more common to go for jobs that would allow them to earn more money.

This shift has a big impact on the way companies hire their employees. It has also created opportunities for recruitment companies to reshape how corporates present themselves to potential candidates.

Another example, we're seeing a big shift from a meat-based diet to a plant-based diet. In the UK, the rate of adoption of vegetarian diets keeps growing year on year. This creates big opportunities for food brands from 100% plant-based sweets (replacing gelatine with plant-based options) to plant-based alternatives to sausages and burgers.

Shifts do not mean that there's going to be a total revolution in the way things are. In the future, we'll certainly still see people willing to work for money beyond any meaning for the type of work they do. We'll also certainly continue to see people happy to have a good rib-eye steak.

Scenarios

> *"A scenario is a story about the future. The details of the scenario may not be true; in fact, they probably are not. But the message may be true—the essence of a plausible future that should be considered and perhaps prepared for."*
>
> – PETER C. BISHOP, Professor of Strategic Foresight

There are moments where you can see critical uncertainties that do not allow you to have a clear view of the future. "The world would be radically different in the situation where Y happens instead of X."

Because of these uncertainties, things are even harder to predict. One solution is to explore the possible outcomes of these uncertainties. You can express these possibilities in the form of different scenarios. Shaping scenarios is about simplifying the large range of things that could happen in the future into just a handful of key possible outcomes.

For example, if you look at the future of the Internet, there's a critical uncertainty around whether it's going to remain centralised (i.e., dominated by the "Amazons" and "Googles" of this world), or whether new regulations and the blockchain technology will make it possible for a more decentralised model (i.e., giving power back to Internet users).

The scenarios should reflect the critical uncertainties you identified. They are a way to envision how the unknown may turn out by creating a set of trajectories. You can then evaluate the probability of each or use that model as a way to anticipate every possible outcome.

Plausible, probable, and preferable

Scenarios must be *plausible*. They have to bring together evidence that makes their occurrence believable. There must be early signals showing that a scenario might happen.

Some scenarios will be more *probable* than others. As creating future scenarios helps you have a view on what may happen depending on how some uncertainties play out, you want the scenarios to cover very distinct possible trajectories. This means that some scenarios will be more likely to happen than others. And this will require you to find ways to assess the probabilities for each scenario.

Once you're in front of a range of scenarios, you'll notice that some scenarios are more *preferable* than others. It's the case either because your company has existing assets and operations that could be threatened by future change, so you will prefer the ones that maintain the status quo. Or it's because you're already attached to a vision or a future idea, so you will hope that the ones that play in your favour will happen.

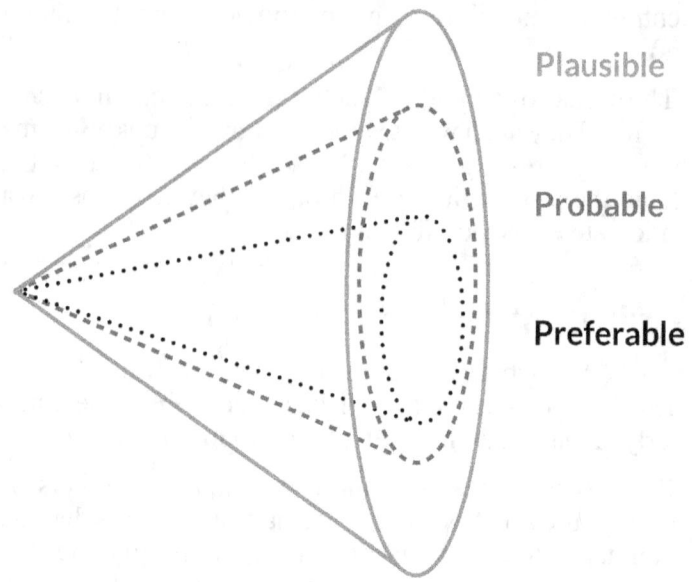

The range of what's plausible will always be larger than what's probable, while your preferred scenarios may be more or less likely—though it's better if they fall under the realm of higher probabilities.

Best case and worst case

In general, scenarios tend to be based on objective variables. The possible outcomes are set based on the uncertainties you identified. In this case, you're not taking into account the perspective of your company and how these scenarios impact your current or future business model.

It can sometimes be helpful to add an element of subjectivity. In that case, you distinguish the scenarios based on how the future may impact your company. You can set apart the negative outcomes and the more positive ones. The best-case scenario amplifies your business model and plays in your favour, while the worst-case scenario poses big challenges for your company.

Having a view on the best case and the worst case can

help you identify the signals, trends, and shifts that you should closely monitor. "If X happens, the landscape may get closer to our worst-case scenario. We should be careful about this."

What happens if it works?

One way to bring scenarios to life is to ask yourself: *"What happens if it works?"* or *"What would happen at scale?"*. Those questions naturally push you to imagine a future where a specific trend takes off and shapes a new paradigm.

The question *"What happens if it works?"* is particularly useful when you look at new technology or emerging cultural trends that have the potential to radically change how things are done or how we live. Indeed, any type of radical change is uncertain. And the challenge is that our minds tend to refuse to imagine a future where something is unlikely to happen. So, if you want to form a view on the future, you need to force yourself to envision what could happen.

There's a lot of stuff going on in the crypto space and the metaverse. Many of these experiments are disturbing because they fit in a new paradigm that barely exists. It's then easy to discard this space as a bubble. Our minds tend to block scenarios that are too far from what we already know. But what happens if it works? In June 2021, a digital-only Gucci bag sold on Roblox for over $4,000. (It's actually more than the physical bag costs.) It could be the effect of speculation, but it could also be a signal. So it's worth asking yourself: "What happens if it works and digital goods become a thing?"

Let me help you push your thinking even further.

Sometimes, a new technology or a new culture is so successful that it takes over everything and replaces older systems. In that case, the question *"What would happen at scale?"* will help you picture a more extreme scenario.

We've seen it with search engines and social networks. At scale, these technologies totally transformed how we buy things. Now, we may be seeing a new wave of change with the rise of social commerce, where shopping becomes a core feature of social media platforms (such as Instagram, Facebook, TikTok, and Pinterest). A large part of social commerce is driven by the content and reviews that influencers and opinion leaders create about products and services. A content creator talks about a product, and by contextualising the benefits, it may.encourage you to buy it through the platform.

As this new marketing and sales channel is gaining momentum, it's worth asking yourself: "What would happen at scale?"

Here's a personal thought process. Influencer marketing is expensive. In most cases, content creators get paid a lump sum to review a product or mention it in the content they share. These are expensive fees that can be complemented with a commission on the sales generated. If you want a decent return on investment, you can't afford selling any type of products through that channel. What you sell must allow for a minimum of margin. Also, influencers who get a commission on what they sell are more incentivised to sell products that have a higher price point.

So, if social commerce were to become the main marketing and sales channel for brands, it's likely that companies will need to focus on having more premium products in their portfolio. In that scenario, brands will need to sell high-margin products that will give them enough flexibility to spend money in influencer marketing, as well as encourage a maximum of content creators to mention their products in the content and reviews they share on social media. This is just a hypothetical scenario. But hopefully, it helps you to see where the question "What would happen at scale?" could lead you.

Mind maps and concept maps

Mind maps and concept maps are diagrams that help you to visually organise information. A mind map delves into a central concept by breaking it down into sub-elements. For example, if you're looking at the tea category, you may want to zoom in on the occasions for having tea.

Exploring occasions for having tea

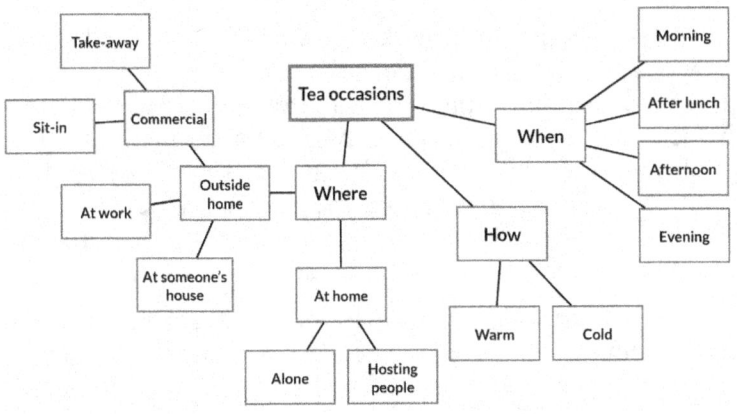

Concept maps are about exploring relationships among different elements. You could use a concept map to explore causality, which can be expressed by the "if this, then that" statement. If you're looking at the future of work, you could map the effects that remote working will have on how we work and how we live.

If/Then: Remote work

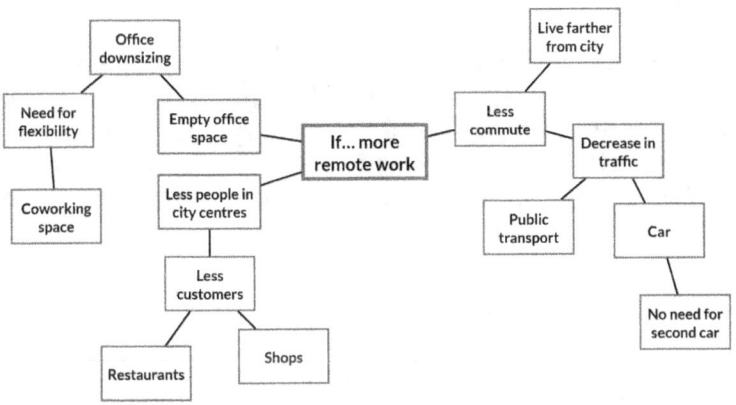

I find these types of diagrams useful to clarify my own thinking or communicate something to an audience.

Storyboards

A storyboard is a way to organise the information visually by highlighting the key moments of a story.

Storyboards tend to look like a comic book with some imagery and captions that describe what is happening in the pictures. They are centred on the protagonists who interact in the future that you foresee. It pushes you to answer a series of questions about that future. What's the story? Whose story is it? Who is there? What are they doing? Where? When? How? It's like standing somewhere in the future and describing what you see around you.

Storyboarding is a tool that you often encounter in the movie industry. It's used to get a feel for the plot of a movie before the movie is shot. In foresight research, storyboards can do two things for you:

First, they can help articulate the data you collected into a coherent view of the future landscape. There's nowhere to hide when you have to illustrate what is happening in a scene, even when it's based on an event that could happen in 10 years. You have to consider smaller details that may have been overlooked so far. By being forced to be as concrete as possible, you may find blind spots or correct some incoherence.

Second, storyboards are excellent to share how you expect things to be in the future. Organising the trends and signals you identified into a visual story will help you tell others about the result of your foresight research. This is useful when you need your company to align on a common thesis.

Additional scanning

Before you start aligning on your thesis about the future, you may have to do some more research and scanning.

Inferring shifts from trends and signals, creating scenarios based on uncertainties and assumptions, and designing mind maps and storyboards… Doing all these things isn't a linear process. It requires a back and forth between organising your thinking and testing it through additional scanning. So make sure to further test your thinking with customers, experts, and potential partners.

Aligning

Once you have formed a compelling view of the future (i.e., an understanding of what could happen that has enough legs to help you spot new opportunities), you must socialise your work and make sure that your company aligns on a specific thesis about the future.

In this section, I want to give you a deeper understanding of what a thesis is and some consideration regarding how you can align internally on a specific thesis.

Shared view

> *"An important factor in thesis-driven investing is that everyone in the firm needs to buy into the thesis or it won't work."*
>
> – FRED WILSON, Partner, Union Square Ventures

Now that you have organised what the future landscapes may look like, it's important to align on a shared view with the rest of your company. *This* is your thesis.

A thesis is the main opinion or theory shared by a group. It's about what you believe the future will look like. It captures the future landscape that you expect to see—the most probable future based on your research.

Having a thesis about the future must act as a North Star for your business. This is the expected future you are preparing yourself for. This is a view of the future landscapes that you will use to spot new business opportunities.

Data vs. beliefs

As you align on a thesis you must make sure that this view is based on data, not just belief. I like how Brad Feld, a startup investor, talks about the distinction between data and beliefs:

> *"I'm fine with 'strong opinions supported by data and experience'. I'm less good with 'strong opinions supported by belief' as I don't really know what underlies "belief" for many people."*

For him, it is critical to have a clear rationale underpinning your opinion—the thesis. Belief is a loose gut feel that is difficult to discuss. Instead, you must have data about signals and trends that back up your view. This will not only reinforce your confidence in the thesis, but also help you align with the rest of your team on that view.

Brad Feld uses a rhetorical question to emphasise this point:

> *"Do you think that is the truth or is that [just] a hypothesis?"*

A thesis must be considered as the "truth" by your team. It's the view on the future landscapes that you will use to spot new opportunities. So, it can't just be an early assumption about the future.

That being said, it doesn't mean you can't revise your thesis later. It's good practice to regularly revise it.

Predictive value

> *"That is not only not right; it's not even wrong."*
>
> – WOLFGANG PAULI, Theoretical Physicist

A thesis must have predictive value. It's a view about the future with a clear logic that supports and explains this view. It must help you anticipate what could happen in the future and should be based on a rationale that can be discussed constructively.

It allows you to do two things:

1. Spot new opportunities by anticipating a possible outcome;
2. Adjust your view of the future by continuously testing your rationale.

It's not about being delusional and believing that you can accurately predict what will happen. It's about having a point of view on *what could happen* and a theory for *why it's likely* that it will happen or why it won't.

Moore's law is a good example of this:

> *"The complexity for minimum component costs has increased at a rate of roughly a factor of two per year. Certainly, over the short term, this rate can be expected to continue, if not to increase. Over the longer term, the rate of increase is a bit more uncertain, although there is no reason to believe it will not remain nearly constant for at least 10 years."*

Trying to predict the future of semiconductors, Gordon Moore spotted a historical trend, observing that the number of transistors in a chip doubled about every year. Ten years later, he revised his forecast stating that it would be doubling every two years.

Your thesis might be proven wrong at some point, but by having a clear rationale you can identify why you were wrong. And this can help you refine how you will foresee the future business environment.

Directionally right

A thesis isn't necessarily about being right in the exact prediction (*accuracy*), but about being right about where the market is going (*direction*).

Being directionally right, especially if you're trying to look at the next 5-10 years, will be enough to spot new opportunities and be confident in seizing them. Whether the market will be growing at 5%, 10%, or 15% does matter. But what's most important is to build confidence that it'll be growing *significantly* because you have a clear rationale explaining why it's likely to happen.

Evidence and warning signs

Your thesis must have predictive value. And this means that it can be further tested. You can come back to it regularly to see if there's any evidence that validates the direction you're anticipating or any warning signs that you were wrong.

It's important to develop a warning system that will allow you to evolve your thesis. Foresight research is an iterative process. While you should avoid changing your mind all the time, you must keep your eyes wide open to update your thesis if you spot warning signs that things aren't going in the direction that you foresaw.

Picking your thesis

> *"Agree and commit, disagree and commit, or get out of the way."*
>
> – SCOTT MCNEALY, Co-founder, Sun Microsystems

It's likely that to pick your thesis, you'll follow the existing decision-making process of your company. I won't dive too much into discussing any type of governance structure. But there are a few things that I'd like to share for consideration.

Make sure that the people involved in picking the thesis have been fully immersed in your foresight research. It's important that they understand the logic, have a good grasp of the forces of change, and fully recognise the critical uncertainties and various possible outcomes.

Be aware that except if you have a small team, a thesis

gets rarely picked by consensus. There's an element of "agree and commit or disagree and commit". Whatever a team member believes, there's a need for everyone to commit to the thesis. It's healthy to have people who disagree, but only if they can voice a clear rationale. It doesn't mean they are right or that they shouldn't follow what the rest of the company decided. You can use their reasoning to build a worthy warning system. But make sure, they are willing to commit to embracing the future that the company foresees.

Investment theses

To bring things to life, I wanted to share some real-world examples with you. One place to look at if you want to find interesting theses about the future is venture capital. Some firms have made their investment theses public, so it's a chance to see what it looks like.

An investment thesis is the overarching strategy of a fund. It's based on what the investment team believes about the future. Startup investors commonly rely on "investment theses" to capture the rationale that guides the investment team when they source new deals and decide whether to make a particular investment.

Let me dive into four examples of investment theses from American and European venture capital firms. Note that these are my interpretations of publicly available information that I have found.

Union Square Venture

Union Square Venture (USV) is a New York-based venture capital firm known for its investments in online platforms and crypto technology. In what they call "Thesis 3.0", USV lays out what the investment team believes about the future and how it influences the types of companies they want to invest in:

> *"USV backs trusted brands that broaden access to knowledge, capital, and well-being by leveraging networks, platforms, and protocols."*

The investment thesis focuses on sectors they think will be critical for the future: "knowledge, capital, and well-being". In the post about the thesis, they further define these points:

> *"Knowledge includes education and learning, but also data-driven insights and access to new ideas. With capital, we include financial capital from financial services innovation, whether in the current system or emerging financial platforms like crypto, but also human capital and technology infrastructure. And with well-being, we think about health and wellness, but also entertainment, connection, community, and fun."*

The thesis also highlights the types of technologies that will be more likely to be transformative: "networks, platforms, and protocols". These are technologies that have real potential to capture value for the long term by "creating an open marketplace" in their sector.

USV also explains the type of business approach that they believe will win in the future:

> *"The goal of these businesses is to build trusted brands—products and services that not only serve a purpose, but integrate into the hearts and minds of their customers in a way that is durable and important. Trust comes from true alignment and convincing the customer that their values and priorities are shared."*

All these elements give the pillar of USV's "Thesis 3.0", which will help the investment team scout for the kind of opportunities that they believe will be important in the future.

Eutopia

Eutopia is a Paris-based firm known for investing in consumer products. Its investment thesis is based on the belief that there's a fundamental cultural shift happening. And this force of change is driving a transformation in the consumer goods sector.

We've reached a pivotal moment where more and more consumers no longer want the mass-produced goods available in supermarkets. They now want to buy from companies that embrace a more sustainable purpose. Its investment team summarises the thesis in a clear single statement:

> *"Good for me, good for society, good for the planet."*

As a result, Eutopia focuses on brands that are rethinking the way we live—how we eat, sleep, dress, exercise, and take care of ourselves. This led Eutopia to invest in companies that do things in new ways such as running no-waste supermarkets, selling healthy meal-replacement shakes, and creating meat alternatives from animal cells to make foie gras.

Andreessen Horowitz

Andreessen Horowitz (a16z) is a Silicon Valley-based venture capital firm that has been a big believer in crypto. Here's how the firm explains the investment thesis of its crypto fund:

> *"Although the Bitcoin whitepaper is now more than 10 years old, we believe we are still early in the crypto movement. Crypto is purely a software movement and doesn't depend on a hardware buildout, in contrast to, say, the internet, which required laying cables and building cell towers. Second, the space is developing extremely rapidly, partly because the code, data, and knowledge is*

> *largely open source, and partly because of the increasing inflow of talent.*
>
> *Finally, we are optimistic because we are deep believers in the power of software. Software is simply the encoding of human thought, and as such has an almost unbounded design space. We find ourselves consistently surprised and excited by the wide variety of creative crypto ideas we encounter. For those of us who have been involved in software for a long time, it feels like the early days of the internet, web 2.0, or smartphones all over again."*

In this extract, the investment team lays out the potential of the technological change underpinned by crypto. In a longer statement posted on their website, they show where they believe change will create the biggest opportunities. This includes: next-generation payments, a modern store of value, decentralised finance, and new ways for creators to monetise their content, products, and services.

Request for Startups

Y Combinator (YC), a startup incubator, created a page on its website called "Request for Startups". On this page, the YC team lists areas where they're interested in seeing more startups. This is where they believe some of the next big opportunities will be.

Here's an extract focused on what they call "Brick and Mortar 2.0":

> *"We are interested in seeing startups that use brick-and-mortar commercial or retail space in interesting and efficient ways.*
>
> *Amazon is putting malls and big box stores out of business. Rather than fighting a losing battle with Amazon, brands need to rethink how to use retail space in ways that play to their strengths. Tesla, Warby Parker, and Peloton, for example, use brick and mortar locations as showrooms that complement their online sales channels. Without the need to store*

inventory, retail space can be used much more efficiently.

Interesting uses of brick-and-mortar space are not limited to retail stores: similar sea changes are happening to restaurants, entertainment venues, local service providers, and office buildings. New businesses will be purpose-built for customers that are trained to expect features like online ordering, deep integrations with other services, and immediate delivery. Flexibility is key. For instance, it is likely that rather than multi-year leases, businesses of the future will utilise "micro-leases" that last days or even hours.

Additionally, the era of big box stores that migrated consumer attention out of main street and into suburban shopping centres flanked by parking lots is likely to change as the era of self-driving begins. Once self-driving cars are adopted widely, our relationship with physical space will evolve in ways that are hard to predict. We want to see startups that are thinking about that shift and building new ways to use physical space."

This example highlights that the team at YC believes that recent cultural, technological, and environmental changes will continue to transform the retail sector, creating opportunities to reshape it. Other topics include theses about carbon removal technologies, cellular agriculture, education, energy, enterprise software, financial services, the future of work, government 2.0, healthcare, improving memory, longevity and anti-ageing, supporting creators, and transportation and housing.

Assessing the circumstances

Even before you align on a thesis, your immediate reaction—as you organise your observations of what could happen in the future—will be to wonder: "This is interesting, but what does it mean for us?"

If you are part of a company—large or small—you will uncover things that will be either boosters or threats of your current business model. And if you are starting a business, my guess is that you already have a rough idea about what you'd like to explore; so you may also try to assess what all this will mean for your nascent business.

Assessing the circumstances to identify the major threats for your business is essential to making sure that your business model and your value propositions remain relevant to your customers and to the changing business environment. This can create a burning platform within your company and push you to react to these upcoming changes.

Having a thesis will help you spot new opportunities, but it will also help you assess the future risks linked to going after an opportunity or another.

CHAPTER EIGHT:

Opportunity Triggers

Once you're aligned on a shared view of the future, you're ready to see how you can uncover new opportunities. To make things practical, I list in this chapter what I call "opportunity triggers".

These triggers bring your focus on the various elements that may cause new opportunities to emerge. They build on the STEER lenses and zoom in on specific aspects of the business environment or of your business model.

Note that this isn't an exhaustive list. Every industry will have its particularities. Also, the triggers aren't mutually exclusive. Some may overlap and lead you to similar opportunities. Again, it depends on your sector.

The point isn't to use these opportunity triggers to do a thorough analysis of the current state of your industry. They shouldn't be overintellectuelised. They are here to stimulate your inspiration. So, let's dig deeper with our opportunity lenses.

Reframe

> *"Since we cannot change reality, let us change the eyes which see reality."*
>
> – NIKOS KAZANTZAKIS, Greek Author

Reframing is a creative exercise. It's about looking at the world with fresh eyes to identify blind spots and broaden your frame of consideration.

I'm sure you'll agree that the longer you've worked in an industry, the harder it is to find ways to do things differently. It's as if everything had already been invented. We've always done it this way or that way. It seems to work, so why should we change it?

As we get more experience about something, we create frames that help optimise the way we think. These frames allow us to be more efficient in what we do, but they also narrow our imagination.

There are two main ways to reframe, and therefore strengthen our creativity:

First, you can challenge your frame of reference by asking "why?" a lot. Exploring the reasons things exist will help you to better understand them. It's a bit like rediscovering this phase of childhood when we ask questions about everything: "Why is grass green?" "Why do dogs bark?" "Why do I have to go to bed now?" Asking "why?" pushes you to approach the world with a beginner's mind. Remember the opportunity mindset of chapter 2?

This can work for redesigning internal processes, but it can also help rethink your value proposition or your entire business model. "Why do we sell our products through a retail network?" "Why is our software not open source?"

Second, reframing can be done by looking at the world from different perspectives. Most of the time, we take an inside-out approach and look at things from our company's point of view.

How often do you truly put yourself in the shoes of your customers or of a partner? Shifting your perspective will help expand your frame of reference. You can even go one step beyond and take the perspective of a competitor or a new entrant. If you were to enter your industry from scratch today, how would you go about it?

Implementing it:

There are a few things you can do to see the world in an entirely different way:

Ask new questions. Assumptions are often baked into the questions we ask. If you ask, "What should we do to plan the birthday party for Jennifer?", you're assuming that you'll celebrate Jennifer's birthday by throwing a party. Now, if you ask, "How can we make Jennifer's day special on her birthday?", you open yourself to a new range of opportunities.

Take a step back. To challenge your questions, you may want to ask yourself: "Why are we doing this that way?" "What's the bigger purpose we're trying to achieve here?"

Go to first principles. A good way to ask new questions and go beyond your assumptions is to go back to first principles. First-principles thinking is about breaking down something into the fundamental parts that you know are true. It could be an opportunity, a proposition, or a business model. What are you absolutely sure is true?

Change perspective. What would Elon Musk say about your industry? How would Apple approach new opportunities? I picked these examples because they have quite extreme ways of approaching things that most people can relate to. Pick anyone or any brand that would help you look at your industry with fresh eyes.

What's new?

As I explained in previous chapters, change is a key trigger for new opportunities. It creates a gap between what people want and what the industry should be able to deliver for them.

You're after long-lasting changes. It could be socio-cultural, technological, economic, environmental, regulatory, or a mix of them. What's important is to figure out how this change will reshape your sector and impact your business model. You also want to get the timing right.

For years, TOEFL and IELTS have dominated the English test sector. Since the 60s, the format has not changed. Taking a test feels like this (based on my own experience and what I have read online):

1. You have to pay about $200 to register;
2. You need to find a time slot that's convenient for you (not that many slots are available because these tests are in high demand so you often have to book months in advance);
3. You must go to one of their official centres (which are usually quite far from home, especially if you live in the countryside, or in a second- or third-tier city);
4. You then take the test on an old PC;
5. If you didn't get the score you hoped for, you have to do it all over again.

It's a model that the two companies behind these tests are reluctant to improve. Despite the Internet making it easy to take tests remotely, they continue to want to make it difficult for the students to go to the centres because this is how they justify such high fees.

But something new started happening:

The rise of new technology, which includes: the Internet, smartphones, and facial recognition. The technological change has enabled Duolingo to launch the Duolingo English Test in 2014. This is an online English test that allows you to certify your English proficiency from home at $49—a more affordable cost than TOEFL and IELTS.

Yet, Duolingo struggled to compete with the incumbents, who had strong relationships with universities. The bottleneck was convincing universities to trust the value of the certificate delivered by the Duolingo English Test.

Duolingo had to wait for an unpredictable event to happen—a wild card—that led to a strong environmental change. Because of the coronavirus pandemic of 2020, most countries went into lockdown. Everything was shut except for essential shops, which means that if you had to take an English test to prove your proficiency level, you couldn't.

Doors opened for Duolingo. Many universities and recruiters started accepting Duolingo's online test. Within a few weeks, the number of people using the Duolingo English Test increased 10 times.

New stuff happened and created a new paradigm and a big opportunity for Duolingo.

Implementing it:

1. Look at your industry through the STEER lenses, i.e., socio-cultural, technological, economic, environmental, and regulatory changes. Any new socio-cultural trends? Any new technology to use? Any new economic context? Any new environmental issues to solve? Any new regulation?

2. What has changed or is about to change that will impact your customers or the way you can create and deliver value to them?

3. Can you spot any gaps between what people want and what can be done?

4. Is there a new paradigm where you would be the only one who could allow your customers to improve their lives?

Where is the niche?

It's difficult to sell something relevant for your customers when you try to be everything to everyone. If you're not specific enough on who should benefit from your value proposition, the risk is to dilute it to such an extent that nobody will find it interesting.

Even the largest brands in the world can't please everyone.

Coca-Cola is the quintessential example of a mass product. It is *the* soda drink that everyone is familiar with. If you think about one brand that can claim to be "mass market", it should be the red can. But the reality is more nuanced.

Let's take the French market as an example. Some sceptics in France don't feel any attachment to the pride for the American Dream, especially those who share the strong identity of being from Brittany. This was an opportunity for creating Breizh Cola, a brand that aims to serve an audience of people who feel a sense of belonging to Brittany—*les Bretons*.

Any brand, any company must be comfortable with telling people "no, sorry… this isn't for you".

Take Apple… They must be doing things right because 95% of business books mention them as a best-in-class example and Interbrand ranked Apple as the most valuable brand in the world. Yet, even Apple doesn't get 100% of the market.

There's a market for those who like the Apple way. And there's a market for those who may want a cheaper phone or computer, or more freedom to customise their devices. Actually, when you look at the smartphone category, Apple has "only" 10 to 15% global market share. Maybe that's Apple that focuses on a niche market. And it seems they are comfortable with that. Apple keeps creating products that feel overpriced but that their target audience loves.

I recently came across a brand of meal replacement shakes for gamers. The concept is tailored to the worldview of the esports community: ideal for an easy-to-eat nutritionally complete meal during a gaming session, created by a professional gamer, and promoted on Twitch and Discord through endorsements by famous video game streamers. The founder saw that there was a new generation of meal replacements (e.g., Feed in France, Huel in the UK) that was becoming a thing. And there was an opportunity to market it more specifically to gamers who do want to eat fast, so they don't need to go "afk" (i.e., away from keyboard) while playing online.

Implementing it:
1. When you look at the overall market, can you identify an underserved group of people?
2. Can you identify a group of people who have distinct needs and desires?
3. Are there people who may feel that they are part of a different culture? People who do not recognise themselves in what the industry offers?

What's the possible bundle or unbundle?

Bundling and unbundling help create value for different customers without having to create something new.

Bundling means packaging multiple small offers into one larger offer so that it feels more attractive for your customers. Combining multiple offers should aim to create value for the customers. It could help reduce the price or make things more convenient. As a rule of thumbs, the more offers are contained in a bundle, the higher the perceived value of the bundle could be.

Unbundling is the opposite. It means splitting up an offer into smaller "more targeted" offers. Here, the value for the customers can come from the simplicity and specificity of the product or service. For a company, it's an opportunity to gain control over a slice of a value proposition.

In the old world of TV, we used to get a subscription from a cable company that would give us access to hundreds of TV channels. This was a *bundle offer*. In the new world of on-demand video, we have to subscribe to a few content providers, e.g., Netflix, Disney +, Prime Video, and HBO, if we want to see all of our favourite TV series. These are *unbundled offers*.

Here's another example:

Craigslist was one of the first businesses that figured out how to make money at scale on the Internet. It brought classified ads online, enabling anyone in the US (and then abroad) to advertise anything.

As the service grew, it started bundling an enormous amount of different types of requests. You could see things like a parent looking for a mathematics tutor, a landlord renting a room, or a comics fan selling a collection of Marvel figurines.

The bundle being so large, it made it difficult for Craigslist to be the best platform for advertising everything. Indeed, you don't advertise tutoring courses in the same way you rent a room or sell vintage clothes.

This created opportunities for unbundling. Other platforms found better ways to serve specific needs. It was the rise of Tutor.com, Airbnb, Fiverr, Upwork, and eBay—among many others. In this case, the bundle offer became big enough to create multi-billion euros opportunities to unbundle.

Implementing it:

1. Can you find bundles that don't seem to work well because the offer is too broad?
2. Can you see competitors who are trying to do everything?
3. Could you do one of the many things they do, but better? Would that create good value for a big enough market?
4. Can a more tailored offer create more value for your customers?

What's the problem?

Looking for "problems that haven't properly been solved yet" is a classic way to spot opportunities.

So what's a "problem"? It's an obstacle that arises in a specific context. Someone is trying to do something but they can't or it's too difficult because of an obstacle. This is the problem.

The opportunity is then to find profitable ways to make it *possible* or *easier* for this person to do what they want to achieve?

Problems can be categorised in big buckets such as time, money, availability, information, and comfort. They can also come from a mix of these categories.

Time

You organised a party. Everyone is having fun, laughing and dancing. There's a good vibe. And suddenly, you realise that there's almost nothing left to drink and eat. *This is the problem.*

In France, delivery companies (e.g., KOL, UberEats, Deliveroo) have jumped on the opportunity to eradicate this problem. You just need to order on their app and the booze gets delivered within 45 minutes. No more empty bottle crisis.

Money

When you're at school, you may need the help of a private tutor. Maybe your teacher isn't great at explaining mathematics, or the way they teach doesn't resonate with your learning style, or you're not paying enough attention, or all of the above... But having a private tutor is expensive. Not everyone has the chance to afford it. *This is the problem.*

And this was an opportunity to create an affordable alternative to private tutoring. Khan Academy does it by offering a catalogue of well-explained online lessons so you can learn at your own pace. (I wish I had access to such a solution when I was at school.)

Availability

When there's a scarce supply of resources, availability becomes an issue. This is the case for recruitment. Finding the right person for a role in your company can be difficult. There are a lot of job ads platforms, but they don't make hiring necessarily easier. *This is the problem.*

Websites like The Muse and Welcome to the Jungle understood that recruitment was broken. Their solution is to give companies a stage to provide "an authentic look at company culture, workplace, and values through the stories of their employees". The platforms help hiring companies talk about the things that matter the most to the younger generations of potential candidates: what impact you will be able to make in your job, who your colleagues will be, how the job will advance your career, how it will feel like to work there, and even what software and technology the company uses.

Information

If you ever had to look for car insurance or an Internet provider, you know there are just so many options that it tends to be overwhelming. And since you've already spent some time digging, the last thing you want is to go for the wrong option. *This is the problem.*

And it's an opportunity to help people choose the best option for them. Money Saving Expert and Compare The Market do this in the UK by giving you the information you need and comparing available options, so you can decide which provider is the best for you.

Comfort

According to Smoon, a startup creating the next generation of menstrual products, women see period panties as as more comfortable than pads or tampons, as they feel like regular underwear and don't cause chafing or irritation like pads can. The founders have heard thousands of women talk about their frustration with the choice of menstrual products on the market. Most options were either uncomfortable, inconvenient, or prone to leaks. *This is the problem.*

It was an opportunity for Smoon create a new kind of period panties designed to be seamless and invisible under clothing, providing comfort and extra protection without bulkiness.

Trust

When you want to download a software, many questions need to be answered. Is it safe? Is it stable so it doesn't make your computer crash when you run it? Is it going to respect your data privacy? There's lots of unknown as to whether a software can be trusted or not. *This is the problem.*

For the iPhone, the solution is the App Store, a centralised distribution platform for apps. Users can download apps from the App Store only if Apple has approved them. This is supposed to guarantee that no malware could be installed on an iPhone. On Android, users tend to rely on the Google Play Store, but they could also use alternatives such as the Amazon Appstore, F-Droid, or the Samsung Galaxy Store.

Implementing it:

1. What frustrates your customers? What do they tell you, if you ask them?
2. What are some problems that you can solve (e.g., time, money, availability, information, comfort, and trust)?
   a. What takes time, but shouldn't?
   b. What's too expensive?
   c. What's not easily available?
   d. What information is difficult to get?
   e. What's not as comfortable as it should be?
   f. What does require extra trust?

What's a problem *you* have?

Another way to find opportunities is to look at problems *you* have. It's somewhat easier because you are the target audience, so you have a clearer view of how big the problem is.

The risk though is that you may be slightly delusional regarding the number of people who care about the topic. So it's important to carefully test that.

At a personal level:

Back in 2010, I was interested in buying T-shirts. It was post-teenage years and I wanted to upgrade my wardrobe. But I couldn't find a brand of T-shirts that was making me feel like "Wow! These guys have thought it through, their T-shirts must be amazing to wear!". I realised that other men were also looking for great T-shirts. Opportunity found! This insight led me to start GoudronBlanc in 2011. Since then, GoudronBlanc has been making great T-shirts that men love to wear.

The problem I personally experienced became a business opportunity. I gained confidence that I was onto something when I figured that I wasn't the only person who complained about this.

At a company level:

Back in 1999, the team at 37signals, a web agency, was struggling to manage their projects via emails. The company couldn't find the right software to run projects and organise the communication internally and with clients. So the team went off to create one. The solution seemed to work well for them, and they realised that other agencies had that same problem. This became their opportunity. So, they called the software Basecamp and started selling it to other agencies and companies.

Basecamp is an example of turning a support function into a product. Selling the project management software has now become the main business of the company that created it. 37signals transformed itself into Basecamp.

Implementing it:

At a personal level...

1. What do you complain a lot about? What problems do you research intensively?

2. What hobbies or categories of things do you spend a lot of money on?

3. What creative activities do you find yourself doing in your spare time?

At a company level...

1. What did you need to create internally to solve a problem that your company was facing?

2. What solutions would make your colleagues' lives or your life easier?

3. What represents a significant budget line for your company?

What seems to be doing well?

Early success from a competitor can demonstrate the existence of a new opportunity for you. It's about using the competition's results as an indicator that something interesting is going on.

If something is working well for them, it could work for you too. Google wasn't the first search engine. The founders saw there was an opportunity for organising the web because they saw early signals of growth for other search engines. Facebook wasn't the first social network. Friendster and Myspace had already demonstrated people's interest in such platforms.

This is something that Costas Markides, professor at London Business School, calls a "fast-second strategy". He distinguishes this from a first-mover and a second-mover strategy.

- A *first-mover strategy* means getting into a market early, hoping that their proposition will become the standard.

- A *second-mover strategy* is more about "wait and

see". It involves waiting until a dominant design has emerged. Once there's a standard, you follow the flow and create a me-too product—a copycat.

- A *fast-second strategy* takes place in between. It's about waiting just enough to identify early signals of traction, but before a standard has been established. It still gives the room to set the standard by defining what the proposition should look like and what its core features are.

The iPhone wasn't the first smartphone, but it defined the dominant design for the smartphone category. Nokia was the first mover. Apple was the fast second. Samsung and Xiaomi are second movers.

TikTok wasn't the first platform allowing us to share short videos, but it defined the standard for sharing short videos. Vine was a first mover. TikTok was the fast-second. Instagram (with Reels) and YouTube (with Shorts) are now following as second movers.

Being fast second works because what matters isn't that you were the first to do something, but that you were the first one to establish a strong positioning in the mind of your audience. As Al Ries, the author of Positioning wrote:

"Marketing is a battle of perceptions, not products."

So if you have something new to say about a product category, something that helps establish a differentiated position in the market, it can work.

Pepsi Cola wasn't the first cola. Marriott wasn't the first hotel chain. Ralph Lauren wasn't the first polo shirt maker. World of Warcraft wasn't the first MMORPG. Signal wasn't the first encrypted messaging service. But in the minds of large audiences, they are all perceived as being first in their category.

Implementing it:

1. Looking at the competition (incumbents and new entrants), what seems to be gaining significant interest among their recent initiatives?
2. What's working well for them that could also be working well for you?
3. Pushing it further: How could you improve it a little bit? How could you improve so it's even ten times better?

Where are there high margins?

It happens that some businesses become so profitable in a sector that it creates new opportunities. It means there's a possibility to undercut them and make things cheaper, to use the high margins to serve the customers better, or both.

This is what Jeff Bezos meant when he said, "their margins are my opportunities," as he was talking about the healthcare sector. This view led Amazon to acquire PillPack, an online pharmacy, which sends you your medication sorted for each day.

There was a compelling business case to challenge the healthcare sector. In 2018—when Amazon acquired PillPack, the average Amazon Prime member spent $1.300, while the average PillPack customer generated $5,000 in revenue.

Another example comes from the eye care sector:

Eyecare is a highly profitable industry led by a handful of companies. In 2010, if you wanted to buy glasses, the average price would have been €300-400. But the cost of making good quality glasses is about €10-40. This type of margin meant there was an opportunity for new entrants.

Many affordable glasses brands popped up around the globe, including Warby Parker (USA), Jimmy Fairly (France), Ace & Tate (Netherlands), and Cubitts (UK). They embraced a direct-to-consumer model that allowed them to sell glasses at a much cheaper price around €95 to €160.

Implementing it:

1. What are the sectors where the products and services seem overpriced?
2. Can you spot businesses that have particularly high margins?
3. If you were able to cut the margins, what could you do to deliver better value to your customers?

What's the value chain like?

The value chain is the set of activities that are moving value from one player to another until it reaches the end-user. It shows the chain of steps that are required to create value by using raw materials, tools, know-how, and energy to create a product or a service.

Often value will move from one player to another until it reaches the end customer.

Before you can buy some Danone yoghurt in a supermarket, the value has to move from the farmer to Danone and its yoghurt factory and then to the supermarket.

This is the value chain at its simplest. The reality is more complex. A yoghurt brand may use a partner to make the yoghurt. The farmer may have bought the cows from a livestock supplier. Maybe the yoghurt factory bought the milk from a middleman? Sometimes the supermarket relies on a centralised procurement service that buys in bulk and dispatches across different supermarket brands to allow some economy of scale.

At each step, there's a player that captures some of the value. So, sometimes, companies want to control several steps—or all the steps—to capture more value. This is what we call a *vertically integrated business model*. In this case, a company manages multiple steps of the value chain—instead of just operating as a manufacturer, a broker, or a retailer.

Here's an example from the "streaming" category:

In 2007, Netflix started its streaming service by licensing a lot of content—movies and TV shows—from distributors such as Disney, Sony, Warner, and CBS. The content providers were happy to license streaming rights as they saw it as an additional source of revenue on top of DVD and cable TV distribution. As Netflix's subscription base grew, the company wanted more of the value chain and started producing original content. It didn't have to only rely on distributors to entertain its subscribers, and it was more profitable to show a Netflix show than pay licensing fees to show a third-party show.

Looking at Netflix's rapid growth, content providers realised that *they* could also take over another part of the value chain and replace Netflix in its role of bridge between the content and the audience. To avoid leaving too much value on the table by relying on others to distribute its catalogue of movies and TV shows, Disney launched in 2020 its own streaming service, Disney+. In parallel, the company has been progressively taking back the streaming rights on its own content.

Depending on your business model, you may or may not want to take part in certain steps of the value chain.

Let's take the example of the oil and gas industry:

Major oil and gas companies—such as BP, Shell, Exxon, and OMV—run a fully integrated business. They interact at each step of the value chain from digging for crude oil (what's called "upstream") to selling the gasoline at gas stations (what's called "downstream").

But they sometimes franchise the operations of gas stations to other businesses. These run just a small part of the value chain: the final distribution at the pump. Franchisees can be an individual running a gas station or a large group that runs a network of stations.

EG Group is a good example of such a network of gas

stations. If you go to the UK, some of the gas stations that sell Esso, BP, Shell, and Texaco fuel could be operated by EG Group. You may see some other brands in the shop next to the forecourt. These could include: KFC, Spar, Carrefour, Starbucks, Burger King, and Subway. While major oil and gas companies try to run activities along the entire value chain, EG Group recognised that there was an opportunity for focusing on the distribution side and adding other services such as Subway sandwiches and Starbucks coffees.

There are pros and cons for both strategies:

- Being fully integrated will always require more capital and capabilities. But it sometimes allows you to better compete, as you have more control over each step of the value chain.

- Focusing on just one part of the value chain can give you more flexibility. It could allow you to be more profitable as you need a different capital structure to run your business. But you will depend more on your suppliers and your partners, and will leave some value to them.

The point is that regularly reviewing each step of the value chain can help you uncover new opportunities. As things are changing, the extent to which you control the overall value chain can be more or less interesting.

Implementing it:

1. What does the entire value chain look like? How has it changed recently? Are there specific steps that you can expect to change soon?

2. Looking at the value chain, is there a step, which you don't control, that concentrates most of the value?

3. Would you be able to deliver more value to your customers if you controlled more steps of the value chain?

4. How could you change your business model to bypass some steps?

What would be a "better" alternative?

In many industries, companies tend to lose sense regarding what "better" means in the eyes of their customers and users. So, identifying what "better" really means can create new opportunities.

For example, I'm thinking about EOS, a body care brand that makes colourful lip balms. Was there a need for lip balms in 2006? Did people have problems finding good lip balms that moisturise well dry lips? Not at all. Lip balms were already ubiquitous.

EOS realised that women (their target audience) didn't need more protective lip balms. What they unconsciously wanted was lip balms that could be used as fashion statements. Lip balms that made their minds feel good (not just their lips). So EOS launched lip balms that had a recognisable design and special scents made with natural and organic ingredients. The opportunity was to discover what "better" lip balms meant to their target audience.

In that case, "better" wasn't "I want a lip balm that's more protective", but "I want a cool lip balm that shows that I'm trendy".

Figuring out what "better" means requires asking questions that no one had asked before. Snapchat is a good example of a company that reframed what a better photo-sharing app would mean. When Snapchat launched in 2011, there were hundreds of photo-sharing applications (including behemoths like Flickr, Facebook, Instagram, and Pinterest). But the founders had found an opportunity to do things differently by asking new questions about what sharing photos meant to us. Why do we send photos? Why do we need to save the photos we share? Why do the recipients need to have a history of the photos they received? Why does a photo-sharing app open with a feed screen and not with a camera screen?

By asking "why?" a lot (remember the section on reframing?), Snapchat's founders were able to uncover a deeper understanding of the psychology around the role of sharing photos in our lives. This led us to see that there was an opportunity to create a "better" kind of photo-sharing app.

Here's another example from the gaming sector:

Let me give you a bit of context to understand how this sector works. The first generation of consoles was launched in the 70s (this includes the Atari Home Pong). And we're now at the ninth generation with the releases in 2020 of the Xbox Series X and Series S and the PlayStation 5.

The video game console category is a tough sector because there can only be a handful of players. It's almost a winner-take-all market. So, every few years, console brands have to launch a new generation of consoles and hope that their latest product will get enough traction.

For the last two decades only three companies—Sony, Microsoft, and Nintendo—have been in a position to fight for the love of gamers.

This era was marked by Microsoft entering the category with the Xbox in 2001 during what was called the sixth generation. It came after the previous successes of the first PlayStation (1995) and the Nintendo 64 (1996), which were part of the fifth generation. The sixth-generation era started with the launch of the Sega Dreamcast in 1998. By 2001, four major consoles were competing including the Sony PlayStation 2, the Nintendo GameCube, and the Microsoft Xbox.

The point I want to make happens at the seventh generation of video game consoles that started in 2005. By that time, Sega had decided to drop the race. Only Sony, Microsoft, and Nintendo were left.

What's noticeable is that both Sony and Microsoft went head to head to fight on performance. The PlayStation 3 and the Xbox 360 were going after great video quality, which at the time was a big thing for hardcore gamers. Nintendo decided to create something "better" for families and people who didn't consider themselves as "gamers". This was the inception of the Wii. The Wii is a world apart from the other two. It doesn't fight on performance but gameplay. The way you play video games with the Wii isn't close to the way you interact with a PS3 or Xbox 360. It's a different kind of "better".

In the eighth generation, Nintendo continued with the same approach. While the PlayStation 4 (2013) and the Xbox One family (2013) focused on performance, the Nintendo Switch (2017) offered a new way of playing allowing people to play their favourite video games in their living room or on the go with the same console. I'm now looking forward to seeing what Nintendo will create to compete with the PS5 and the Xbox Series X—the ninth generation. But what's interesting to note is that even if the Nintendo Switch is considered to be part of the eighth-generation era due to lower processing power, it remains competitive with the ninth generation.

We tend to be so proud of our products and services and so focused on matching the competition that we often overlook the criteria that matter most to our customers. Rediscovering what "better" means can be a great source of opportunities.

Implementing it:

1. What criteria do your customers use to decide between your proposition and the alternative ones? What does matter most to them?

2. Why do your customers need your product or service? What else can you do to help them achieve their goals?

3. How does your competition evaluate the performance of their propositions?

4. What aspects and criteria are essential in the eyes of the audience, but seem to be neglected by your competitors?

What's the most profitable segment?

Sometimes, it is better to leave part of the market to your competitors. The reason is that there are segments that are more profitable to serve than others.

There's an interesting case in point in the insurance sector. If you want to launch a new car insurance company, you're better off selling policies to good drivers and leaving your competition to cover people who are more at risk to make a claim.

In practice, things aren't that simple, because regulation can make it difficult for insurers to discriminate among insurees. But it sometimes works. For example, Health IQ, an American insurance company, claims that "people with healthy lifestyles are overpaying for life insurance". But "living a healthy lifestyle is associated with a significantly lower risk of early death, heart disease and type 2 diabetes". On their website, they highlight that it makes sense that "people with healthy lifestyles" should pay less for their life insurance. What the company attempts to do is to attract people who have less risk of having health issues. And obviously, this segment is much more profitable for a life insurance company because these people are less likely to get ill.

The luxury industry works in the same way. Givenchy, Dior, or Burberry sell their products to a much more profitable segment. It costs more to reach and sell to someone who buys luxury products, but they are more profitable to serve than someone who prefers *fast fashion* clothing.

"Real aficionados" can also be a more profitable segment to serve. For example, a high-quality chocolate brand can succeed in getting chocolate lovers to buy directly online, while most people wouldn't bother. As a result, the brand wouldn't have to compete with Hershey, Cadbury, or Nestlé in the supermarket.

It's just not true for chocolate. The same could apply to jeans lovers, tea lovers, coffee lovers, bike lovers, calligraphy lovers, and so on. The list is endless. Also, real aficionados tend to buy more and do this more often. They tend to be more loyal to brands who deliver on their expectations, and can be great ambassadors.

Serving the *most profitable segment* requires a different cost structure, different priorities, but it can be a much more profitable segment to focus on.

Implementing it:

1. What segments of your market are the most profitable to serve?
2. What would "luxury" or "real aficionados" mean in your sector?
3. How different are their expectations? What would "better" mean for them?

What's threatening an existing business?

> *"One of [Steve] Job's business rules was to never be afraid of cannibalising yourself. 'If you don't cannibalise yourself, someone else will,' he said."*
>
> – WALTER ISAACSON, Author

STEER-type of change can be a threat to an existing business model. You may see some of your customers leaving for the competition because they can better serve them in these new circumstances.

You need to put yourself in a position where you can anticipate these future threats and turn them into opportunities. Most of the time, it's about catching them early enough so you can adapt on time.

Meta has repeatedly been able to turn threats into opportunities:

- In 2012, when Instagram started taking over the photo-sharing space, Meta was quick to acquire the business.

- As Snapchat started becoming a dominant social media player, Meta decided to compete with Snapchat's sharing feature by launching Instagram Stories (2016) and Facebook Stories (2017).

- In 2020, TikTok became a strong competitor as a video social platform. This pushed Meta's Instagram to launch Reels, a video browsing feature that imitates the way you can consume content on TikTok.

Microsoft went through a similar journey:

The rise of software-as-a-service and collaboration apps threatened Microsoft Office. Google Docs, Dropbox, and Slack were starting to eat into Microsoft's place. As a response, the company built a new ecosystem around its Teams app, fostering online teamwork through chat, file sharing, and collaborative real-time editing.

Both Meta and Microsoft used signals of threats to spot new opportunities to grow their business—even if it meant cannibalising certain elements of their existing business model.

Implementing it:

1. What could a competitor do to outcompete your company?

2. What new STEER change could be a threat to your business?

3. If you were to start from scratch now, how would you do it? Same technology? Same business model? Same customers? Same branding?

What's not going to change?

Let me start this section with a somewhat provocative quote from Jeff Bezos:

> *"I very frequently get the question 'What's gonna change in the next 10 years?' I almost never get the question 'What's not going to change in the next 10 years?' And I submit to you that that second question is actually the more important of the two, because you can build a business strategy around the things that are stable in time."*

While change is a driving force for creating new opportunities, things that won't change are a strong foundation for a long-lasting opportunity.

I find that this quote from Bernard Arnault, the CEO of LVMH, truly illustrates that point:

> *"In 20 years people may not have iPhones but they will still be drinking Dom Perignon."*

The STEER lenses are a good tool to guide your attention and help you notice what is changing. If you want to look at what won't change, you can focus on the elements that are core to our human nature. These aren't likely to change too soon. For that Maslow's hierarchy of needs is a great starter that will help you consider our fundamental human drives.

As humans, we all have needs for health, needs for safety, needs for love and belonging, needs for self-esteem and status, and needs self-actualisation.

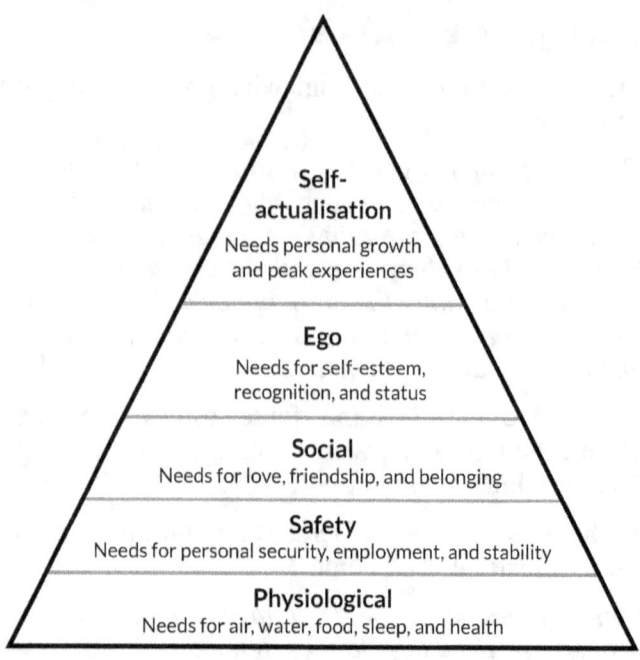

This framework works like a ladder. Once the most basic needs are fulfilled, we try to fulfil high needs. Maslow explains the progression this way:

> *"It is quite true that man lives by bread alone—when there is no bread. But what happens to man's desires when there is plenty of bread and when his belly is chronically filled? At once other (and 'higher') needs emerge and these, rather than physiological hungers, dominate the organism. And when these in turn are satisfied, again new (and still 'higher') needs emerge and so on."*

The modern expression of our desires is rooted in some fundamental needs. While you can observe that what people want changes over time, at a deeper level this is all based on our fundamental needs.

Implementing it:

1. What are some fundamental needs and desires that your audience will always have? What is the modern expression of these needs?

2. How can they meet these needs in more satisfying ways?

3. How do people behave once they have fulfilled those needs? What's the next step?

What would be contrarian thinking?

A contrarian is someone who has a reason to challenge conventional wisdom. It's someone who sees potential in what could seem counterintuitive. It's about holding little known insight: "I understand something about the world that others do not."

On 25th November 2011, businesses were busy with the frenetic start of Black Friday. ON the same day, Patagonia, an eco-friendly outdoor clothing brand, put a full-page advertisement in the New York Times. The ad pictured a Patagonia fleece jacket with the title "DON'T BUY THIS JACKET".

Here's an extract of the advert:

> *"Black Friday, and the culture of consumption it reflects, puts the economy of natural systems that support all life firmly in the red. [...] We want to do the opposite of every other business today. We ask you to buy less and to reflect before you spend a dime on this jacket or anything else."*

The ad was an expression of Patagonia's contrarian view. While most fashion brands cut prices so you can buy more, Patagonia seemed to believe that there are people who care about the environment and want to buy from brands that do everything they can to limit the impact of consumption on the planet.

The opportunity for Patagonia was to fill the gap

between mass consumption and a growing awareness of the negative impact of consumerism. The advert was just one illustration of what the team at Patagonia does to position itself far from the fast fashion trend.

Here's a recent case of contrarian thinking:

Substack is an online platform that "makes it simple for a writer to start an email newsletter that makes money from subscriptions". Such a business generates revenue in a way that often follows a Pareto model: 20% of the writers help generate 80% of the revenue.

For this to work, you need to attract well-known writers who will then attract a lot of subscribers. The contrarian assumptions from Substack are that:

- Writers who are used to being well paid by renowned newspapers and magazines to publish their work will prefer to go independent, taking entrepreneurial risks and having to own the responsibility to attract and keep subscribers;
- Subscribers will be happy to pay to follow the work of independent writers instead of or in addition to paying for their favourite magazine and newspaper subscriptions.

Substack launched in 2018. At the time of writing, it's been only a few years. But, it seems that the company's growth is following a trajectory that is proving them right. There's still a question about the tipping point: Will it remain niche or will it reach a tipping point allowing the business to scale massively? But overall, their contrarian approach to the traditional media world seems to have unearthed a valuable opportunity.

When I talk about contrarian thinking, there's always a thought that comes to mind: It's that there is a thin line between what we could call "genius" or "insanity". (And this is true that in most cases, we rely on how things turned out, as a way to decide between the former or the latter.

But there's a solution!

Remember the mindset of proactively experimenting. If your opportunity is triggered by some heavy contrarian thinking and everyone is calling you "crazy", you may want to dig for more signals and evidence that you are right. This may involve low-cost experimentation that will help you and your team gain confidence in the logic of your contrarian thinking.

Implementing it:

1. What are the main assumptions made in your sector? What's held as a precious truth that you could challenge?
2. How could you challenge what everyone believes about your sector?
3. What do contrarians say in your industry?

What would counterbalance the major trends?

The idea behind countertrends is that for every major trend, you can see a trend going in the opposite direction.

There's a tension here. On the one hand, we have a tendency to mirror others and do things that make us feel part of the zeitgeist. On the other hand, we have a desire to be different and feel unique. The latter is a key driver of countertrends. It's triggered by people who do not agree with what the majority is doing. And it is strengthened by a feeling of "us versus them".

When the majority seems to go in one direction, you can often see a growing "countertrend minority" reacting to this and doing the opposite. These aren't people who are lagging behind the trend. Instead, they are reacting to a growing trend. And they may actually be ahead of the next wave.

- Fast fashion is trendy. You see a lot of people buying lots of cheap clothes. But you also see a few people caring about the quality and the origin of the clothes they wear.

- Hypermarkets are trendy. You see a lot of people doing their grocery shopping in industrial areas. But, you also see a few only buying from the local shops and the farmers market.

- SaaS has been a trendy way to offer software services connected to the cloud. You'll see lots of companies adopting it because it's convenient, but you'll see companies going away from it because they may have trust issues with having all their data in a third-party storage service.

Thinking about countertrends could get you in the same spot as contrarian thinking. The thinking process is a bit different though. While contrarian thinking may unlock something that goes against what people commonly assume in an industry, countertrends are about looking at counter-reactions to a major trend.

Most of the time, looking at countertrends leads to niche businesses—small but still good businesses. But sometimes, the countertrend overtakes the underlying trend.

Implementing it:

1. Looking at the major forces of change, what would the market do if it was reacting in the opposite direction?

2. What opportunities could the countertrends create?

3. What do some people do that appears to be done in reaction to a major trend?

What's a smoother user experience?

Getting rid of friction in the user journey can create a real competitive advantage. A system that's easy to use can be super attractive and a compelling reason to switch to a new system. When all the products and services on the market are complex and feel overwhelming for the people who use them, there's an opportunity for making their lives easier.

In B2B, a better user experience tends to increase productivity and makes working together so much easier. Google Docs and Trello are good examples. It just flows.

In B2C, a smooth user experience feels intuitive. No questions asked. No need for a user manual. It's almost as if you've always been using the product or service. It's like the iPhone. Have you seen a child use an iPhone? In minutes they know how to use it—often years before they learn how to read.

One of the reasons Zoom gained millions of users is that it simplified the user experience. Most video call softwares required its user to have a sort of ID before joining a call. This could be a phone number (e.g., WhatsApp) or an account (e.g., Skype).

Zoom changed that. It removed a large chunk of the friction for joining a video call. You didn't need an account, an app, or a phone number to join a Zoom call. A link and a web browser were enough. By making it so easy to join, Zoom became a compelling option for people who wanted to organise group calls for a business meeting or a family gathering. Even someone's grandparents could figure out how to click on a link that was sent in an email.

Casper transformed the way we buy a mattress by removing friction in the customer experience. The company proved that you don't need to go to a shop and sit on a mattress to decide whether you want to buy it. You can figure things out online and get your mattress delivered at home. Casper created a smoother experience by making it so easy to buy bedding online that it gained lots of traction and established a new standard in the sector.

At the end of the day, it's hard to imagine what it was like before the great user experience existed. A slick user experience makes a product or a service so simple (and sometimes fun) to use. It just feels satisfying.

Implementing it:

1. What's so annoying or difficult to use?

2. How can you make it so simple to get the job done? How could you get rid of any steps?
3. What can you do to encourage users to come back and use your product or service over and over again?
4. Could you hide advanced features so that new users have an easier onboarding?

What would be a great partnership?

Great opportunities can also arise from a partnership between brands. The rationale is that compounding one brand with another can give a broader reach and helps appeal to a larger audience.

In recent years, the fashion industry has demonstrated the value of collaboration across brands. There's an endless list of examples.

When Balenciaga creates Crocs shoes or Rick Owen works with Birkenstock, all these brands are using each other's assets to show a new expression of their brand universe. It's an opportunity to extend the brands' footprint. Tactically, it's also a way to create some new news and get some PR.

Supreme, a streetwear pioneer, made a name for collaborating with a broad range of brands. This includes Louis Vuitton bags, a New York Times cover, a Fender Stratocaster guitar, and even some Everlast boxing gloves.

Celebrities have played the game too. Though this type of collaboration is often limited to showing celebrity endorsement, there are some good examples of long-lasting partnerships: Michael Jordan x Nike with the Air Jordan and Rihana x LVMH with Fenty.

Brand partnerships often address our needs for status, belonging, and recognition. "People like us do things like that." But partnerships aren't just about branding, it can also be about unlocking new distribution channels and new capabilities.

When you visit a BP gas station in the UK, you may have noticed an M&S Simply Food shop in the backcourt. This is the result of a partnership that started in 2005. BP operates more than 300 M&S shops. For M&S, it's an opportunity to broaden its reach across the UK. For BP, it's a way to offer more products to those who stop to refuel their cars, and therefore make more money per customer.

Though they can be difficult to negotiate, partnerships are effective to create new opportunities. Some may be quite tactical, but there's always a chance to turn this into long-lasting strategic moves.

Implementing it:

1. What are you missing that a partner could provide?
2. What other brands and businesses could be complementary to yours? What value would this create?
3. What special capabilities, insight, and unique brand expression would you bring to the mix?
4. What would you hope to build that creates value for your customers—or theirs?

What can be done with existing assets?

In 1997, when the low-cost airline Ryanair chose Beauvais-Tillé as its hub in France, all the other airlines were relying on Charles de Gaulle and Orly Airport—two airports that are much closer to Paris.

Ryanair saw in the small Beauvais airport an *under-utilised asset*. Though it is much farther away from Paris than the other two Parisian airports, Ryanair believed this could be appealing to many travellers if the airline was able to offer low fares and a good bus connection. They also renamed the airport to Paris-Beauvais to give the impression that it wasn't that far (even though it is roughly 70 km from Paris).

In 1996, 64,000 passengers flew through Beauvais airport. 20 years later, the airport was welcoming nearly 4 million passengers.

Ryanair reframed what it meant to travel. It wasn't about faster or more comfortable, but cheaper. "Can you get me to my holiday destination cheaply, please?" The airline could only make it work because they had identified an under-utilised asset.

Implementing it:

1. List all the tangible and intangible assets your company has. Which assets could you use and monetise in other ways?

2. What assets that you could buy or get access to seems to be under-utilised?

What can you do to participate in a flourishing ecosystem?

Jonah Peretti, a co-founder of The Huffington Post, started BuzzFeed in 2006. At the time, this was a side project focused on building an algorithm that curated articles that seemed to gain virality online. The premise was that the media landscape was changing. Jonah progressively realised that the Internet, social networks, and mobile transformed the way we consume news and entertainment.

Very early on, BuzzFeed was able to successfully capture value from the growing virality that Facebook's News Feed had been creating. BuzzFeed's content was gaining great exposure on Facebook, allowing the website to build a large audience of young readers.

What Jonah Peretti realised is that a new ecosystem had transformed expectations in terms of content consumption. A new paradigm was born. Younger readers wanted different formats that were more social, interactive, easy to browse, and entertaining or smart. From the start, BuzzFeed was designed to participate in the new web ecosystem.

Implementing it:

1. What ecosystems could help you reach an audience that is already highly engaged?
2. Are there any ecosystems that could help accelerate the development of your product or service?
3. How can you create value for the ecosystem while capturing part of the value that you create?

In practice

It's likely that a great business opportunity answers several of the trigger questions. Again, the list is here to bring some inspiration to spot potential opportunities, it's not a MECE (mutually exclusive, collectively exhaustive) framework.

For example, a "what's better" opportunity can emerge from a personal problem that is also looking at a sector with high margins and could threaten an existing business.

Let me illustrate that with Dyson's first product: a bagless vacuum cleaner. Annoyed by the poor suction of the vacuum cleaner he owned, James Dyson went on a journey to invent a better alternative. Thanks to his persistence as well as engineering and design genius, James Dyson was able to create a remarkably better and nice looking vacuum cleaner.

At first, James Dyson wanted to licence the technology to vacuum cleaner brands so that they could benefit from the innovation and manufacture it at scale. But he kept getting "no" as an answer. The companies weren't keen on adopting the new technology because that totally changed and threatened their existing business model. It was putting at risk a model that relied on selling affordable vacuum cleaners and making a high margin on the bags. The "refill" or Gillette model that is known in the shaving and printing sectors, whereby the companies make a recurring revenue by selling a component that is necessary to use the machines they make and sell.

Ultimately, Dyson didn't licence the technology and

went on manufacturing the vacuum cleaner itself, and selling it through retailers and its own website. Since then, the company has triggered a huge shift in the vacuum cleaner sector by making the bag model feel obsolete in the eyes of the market.

Read the opportunity triggers again and you'll see that a few of them could lead to the opportunity that James Dyson was able to seize. Of course, this is an ex-post analysis. But, hopefully, it helps bring things to life so you have a clearer picture of how you can use the opportunity triggers as inspiration.

CHAPTER NINE:

How to decide

It's likely that by using the STEER framework and the opportunity triggers as inspiration, you'll spot multiple opportunities. Once you look at the world with the right lenses and the appropriate mindset, you realise the wealth of potential opportunities that are out there.

You could even find this daunting. There's just so much out there. Life's too short. Resources are too limited. One cannot focus on everything.

So, you need to choose. You need to decide.

Some opportunities may not be big enough. Some may not be right for you and your company. Others may be too complex to tackle. And there are some that may be interesting now, but they won't last long enough.

Now it's time to talk about strategy. As Michael Porter said, "the essence of strategy is choosing what not to do."

Here I will share some considerations on how to decide on what business opportunities to go after. For that, let's wear some nice strategic lenses.

Not just science

> *"Although our intellect always longs for clarity and certainty, our nature often finds uncertainty fascinating."*
>
> – CARL VON CLAUSEWITZ, Military Theorist

There's no exact science to decide on whether to pursue an opportunity.

Yes... You can assess the market potential, estimate your fair share, discount future cash flow and look at your net present value (NPV), calculate the breakeven point, evaluate the risks, and do some sensitivity analysis. But all these things won't decide for you.

The decision-maker could be an entrepreneur, a team of founders, one or several managers, the CEO, or the board members. But ultimately, whether there's a structured decision-making process or not, the decision will rely on "informed intuition".

If it was pure science, we would have a formula and algorithms making decisions for us. Strategy would be entirely automated.

The reality is that "it might not work". There's always risk involved when you make a *strategic* decision, i.e., the decision you make when you say "yes" to one thing and "no" to an endless list of other things.

Decision making is a broad topic and if you work for a large company, most of the governance structure will already be in place. That being said, there are ways you can better inform the existing decision-making processes, so in the following sections, I will lay out some food for thoughts.

Both external and internal

> *"Find something that is both important to you and resonates with a group of people at this particular moment in time."*
>
> – D'ARCY COOLICAN, Investment Partner, Andreessen Horowitz

Do you remember the short description of "opportunity" I shared at the start of the book?

> *"An opportunity is a set of circumstances that opens the door for you to make something that will create value for others, so that you may get a profitable return in exchange."*

These circumstances are both external and internal to your company. An opportunity appears when *external circumstances are right*, and right *for your company*. That's because opportunities are subjective. What's right for your company may not be right for another company.

So when you decide on going after an opportunity, you need to explore both external factors (*the business environment*) and internal factors (*your company*).

Right business environment, right for *your* company

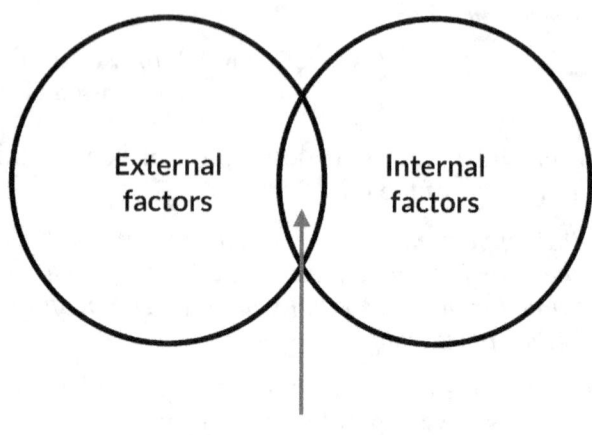

Your opportunity

In the coming subsections, I'll unpack a framework that covers the most important factors to take into account. This isn't an exhaustive list, but it's a good starter to help you assess possible opportunities.

It's difficult to be specific because it depends so much on the kind of business that you run. I will cover some ground, but you'll need to build on what I share here to have a framework that fully suits your company.

External factors = The business environment

External factors shape the business environment where the company could play. It's about the market, i.e, the customers and the users. And it's about the industry, i.e., the suppliers, the competitors, the partners, and all the other stakeholders that play a role in the ecosystem.

For this, you need to have spotted a need or desire in the market (*desirability*) that isn't already taken care of by too many players (*competitivity*), and where you won't get squeezed by suppliers and the broader ecosystem (*complexity*), while making sure that you can legally and contractually pursue that opportunity (*legality*).

Desirability

Desirability focuses on how much the market needs or wants something. It's also about the potential size of the market and how it could evolve over time.

Here are a few questions to help you assess desirability:

- What is your target market? Are there attributes you could use to identify your future customers? Demographic, psychographic, or behavioural attributes?

- What is the market size? What is the growth potential of the market? Why is it going to grow? Can you identify forces of change that will accelerate and sustain the growth?

- How much would they spend? What is their willingness to pay and price sensitivity? Can you define how much your audience spends on alternatives to what you could offer? Are there proxies you could rely on?

- How frequently would they spend? Can you think of occasions of purchase or consumption? What's the trigger for the need or desire?

It's important to be as specific as possible. Your target market isn't the whole market, so you need to find ways to define it in a way that is practical to reach them with your future product or service.

For example, the market size for jeans is huge. Billions of jeans are made every year. But it's so fragmented. So how did Naked & Famous Denim, a clothing brand known by aficionados for using unique and rare denim fabrics from Japan, approach it? For sure, they didn't think: "Whoa! Let's get 1% of the jeans market." Instead, they identified a demand for high-end jeans, i.e., an audience of people who like wearing well-crafted products. This audience is much smaller than "billions of jeans". But it also comes with a specific willingness to pay and price sensitivity.

The good thing for Naked & Famous is that more and more people want to go away from the fast fashion model because of rubbish design, poor fabric, and the negative impact on the environment. They were keen on buying from brands that made great clothes and had good stories to tell. This was the opportunity for Naked & Famous.

Competitivity

> *"We think in terms of that moat and the ability to keep its width and its impossibility of being crossed as the primary criterion of a great business. And we tell our managers we want the moat widened every year."*
>
> – WARREN BUFFETT, CEO, Berkshire Hathaway

Competitivity requires you to assess the current and potential competition. It's also about evaluating the competitive pressure and how long you can keep them away from being better than you at serving your customers.

- How fierce is the existing competition? Are a lot of companies going after the same opportunity? How big are your competitors? How well established are they?

- How do you position yourself against the competition? How fast can they catch up?

- How difficult will it be to get your competitors' customers to switch to your future proposition?

- How fast will the competition be able to catch up?

- Would the incumbent catch up? Could new startups easily join the party? What alternatives could replace your future proposition?

- What will your "economic moat" be? Can you create a competitive advantage that is difficult to mimic? What will the barrier to entry be? Are there high switching costs? Is it heavily regulated?
- How obvious is the opportunity? Is there a lot of hype? Is the competition clear on how to go after the opportunity?
- Is it a zero-sum game? Is it a winner-take-all market? Is it a situation where all competitors can grow the market together?
- Is it a situation where you have frenemies, i.e., competitors who also help you build your own proposition?

One key consideration is whether you're in a zero-sum game or a win-win game situation.

The smartphone industry is a good example of a zero-sum game. Once someone has bought a phone, it's unlikely they'll need another before a while. One company sold a phone. Its competitors didn't; they lost the sale.

In contrast, the podcast sector is more in a win-win game situation. Someone who listens to a podcast won't just listen to one podcast series. They'll likely look for other podcasts to listen to. If you run a podcast, you can benefit from recommending other podcasts. Your fellow podcasters are in the same situation. They won't lose much by recommending your podcast. Quite the contrary, if the recommended podcasts are good, the listeners will be happy to get the recommendations.

Complexity

Complexity is about the difficulty to navigate the ecosystem and negotiate with potential suppliers and partners. The more difficult it is for your company to get access to the raw materials, tools, products, and talent, the more complex the business environment is.

- How difficult is it to navigate the ecosystem? Is it a "safe" space or a "dangerous" one?
- What is the relationship between the competition and your potential suppliers?
- Is there an ecosystem that can facilitate access to new technology?
- How easy is it to hire people in that sector?
- What does the value chain look like?
- How many suppliers could you rely on? Is there just one supplier? What happens if your supplier goes out of business?
- Where are the best suppliers located?
- How much trust can you put in the suppliers? Could they copy you? Could they disclose sensitive information to your competitors or the public?
- How easy is it to negotiate with the suppliers? Can they drive the cost up without notice?

The right model depends on your company and on the type of industry you're in. There are cases where it pays out to have a lean business model and rely on many partners. In other cases, it could be better for your business to be fully integrated.

The grooming brand Harry's is a good example of vertical integration. In 2013, the company began selling razors with a direct-to-customer model. Just 10 months into their journey, the startup acquired a 93-year-old German razor factory for $100 million. The reason? The co-founders wanted to control manufacturing. This was a way for the company to bulletproof their business model. There are only a few places in the world that make high-quality blades. By owning the factory, Harry's made sure they wouldn't risk seeing the competition relying on the same supplier or losing their supply chain because a big brand would have acquired the factory.

Legality

Legality is about being in accordance with the law. This includes any national or local regulations, but also contracts between your company and third parties. This may sound obvious. Rare are those who decide to go after an opportunity that would be illegal (or maybe not that rare…). But the reality is that not every rule is black or white.

You see that there's a good opportunity for milk alternatives. People do see themselves putting almond-based or oat-based alternatives to replace milk in their bowl of cereal. But if you can't call these "almond milk" or "oat milk" because the food regulations ban these terms, would it be such a good opportunity? Do people find oat drinks or almond beverages appealing?

- What does the regulatory framework look like? Are there laws that would limit your ability or prevent you from going after the opportunity?
- What data privacy and safety rules will you need to comply with?
- Would your move put you at risk to fall under competition and antitrust regulations?
- What contracts or clauses would limit what you can do (e.g., non-compete clause and NDA)?
- Would pursuing the opportunity require a move into a regulated industry (e.g., healthcare or banking)?

Laws and regulations are the obvious suspects. But contracts and agreements can often be a big limiting factor when you are considering going after a new opportunity.

In 2018, the sales of energy drinks reached €3 billion in the US. This represents a significant opportunity for a soda company like The Coca-Cola Company. But by that time Coca-Cola didn't have a branded energy drink.

Coca-Cola Energy was launched only in 2019, but not without pain. Days after the launch, The Coca-Cola

Company got haunted by a ghost, a non-compete clause that dated from 2015. That year, Coca-Cola had acquired shares in Monster, the famous energy drink brand. Part of the deal was a non-compete agreement roughly stating that Coca-Cola couldn't launch a branded energy drink that competes with Monster.

So when Monster heard about the launch of Coca-Cola Energy, their legal team wasn't happy. The case went to arbitration. It was solved when the arbitrators ruled that "Coca-Cola Energy products fall within an exception to a non-compete provision relating to beverages marketed or positioned under the Coca-Cola brand".

The story shows the importance of contracts in assessing the legality of an opportunity, but also how grey legality can be. While Monster read something in the contract, Coca-Cola was reading something else. Because of their misalignment, they had to find a solution in arbitration.

Internal factors = Your company

While external factors tell you whether there's an opportunity to do something, internal factors tell you whether there's an opportunity for *you,* for *your* company.

This is about your business model, your operational capabilities, and your general strategy, i.e., what you can profitably do now and the directions that your company is taking.

Looking at the internal factors will push you to consider how your company may go after each potential opportunity with some ideas of potential products or services. You need a rough idea of what you could do in order to assess whether it's possible (*feasibility*), how it will play out financially (*viability*), and whether it fits with your existing strategy (*identity*), while making sure you're not putting all the eggs in the same basket (*optionality*).

Feasibility

Feasibility is about the ability of your company to seize the opportunity. Are you able to do it? This question has big repercussions on the financials—and therefore the "viability" factor.

- How much of your existing assets and capabilities will you be able to use?
- Will you need new skills? Will you need to hire new people?
- Could you partner with third parties and suppliers to make it happen?
- Can you rely on existing suppliers or do you need to find new ones?
- Does your brand fit with the opportunity? Is your brand recognised for serving similar needs and desires?
- How much R&D would be required to make it happen? How long before you can ship something good enough for your customers?

Going after an opportunity always creates feasibility challenges. Some are big, others much easier to overcome. But sometimes, changes that seem mundane from the customer's perspective can be difficult to implement.

For Mars, it was radically more difficult to go after the opportunity to broaden its brand into the ice cream category with Mars ice cream, than to go after the protein trend by launching Mars protein bars. I can acknowledge that adding proteins to the ingredients of Mars bars without altering the taste may have been challenging. But Mars could still rely on the same factory and supply chain. To launch Mars ice cream, Mars had to create new technical capabilities to make the ice cream and transport it in refrigerated trucks. It may have relied on partners to do so without creating too much upfront cost, but it was a whole new set of challenges for the marketing, R&D, and logistics.

Viability

Viability deals with the topics related to the financials of the business model. At the most basic level, an opportunity must deliver more revenue than it costs to go after it. But there's also a question of opportunity cost. What else could you have done with this time and money?

- What's the market potential? What market share could you have? What's your fair share?
- How much would it cost to seize this opportunity now? How much would it cost in the future?
- What would be the possible cost structure for this? How much fixed costs? How much variable costs? Can you scale with little marginal costs?
- What are the possible business models? Would the opportunity require a major shift of your existing business model?
- What is the expected return for the opportunity?
- What is the opportunity cost? Are there other opportunities that can deliver better returns?
- How could you lower the upfront investment required?
- What are the synergies that could make the opportunity more financially interesting?

Before 2013, if you wanted to use Photoshop, a photo and graphic editor created by Adobe, you had to buy a CD or download the software and pay about 1,000 euros for it. Adobe relied on a model based on customers having to pay a lump sum for a version of the software. If a customer (often a company) wanted a more recent version, they had to pay another lump sum upgrade.

Now, Adobe relies on a different model. It moved to a software-as-a-service model, where its customers subscribe to use Photoshop. They no longer own the right to a licence, but have to pay a monthly fee of about 60 euros per month for Photoshop. This is a major shift in their business model.

While Adobe was used to get paid lump sums with just upfront development costs associated, it is now in a model where it rents server space from Microsoft Azure, regularly updates its software, and has to make sure its customers often use Photoshop so they keep paying their subscription. The cash flow is more predictable, but users can now cancel at any time, so Adobe has to make sure they continuously deliver value to their customers. They moved from evaluating cost/benefit for each version to a continuous delivery model where you may not get instant rewards for large investments.

Identity

> *"Every advertisement should be thought of as a contribution to the complex symbol which is the brand image."*
>
> – DAVID OGILVY, Advertising Man

Consistency plays a strong role in the success of your company. While it's important to know when to adapt and change gear, it's also key to keep a certain level of coherence among the things that a company does.

In this case, it means that the opportunity you choose must contribute to supercharging the company's overall strategy, building on existing strengths. To win in the long term, your company needs to focus on projects that reinforce the current position of your company.

But it's not just about being consistent with what your company does, it's also about being true to the people who work in the company. It would be difficult to successfully go after an opportunity that doesn't energise your people, or worse that forcefully clashes with your company's values. Going after an opportunity that gets people excited will put all the chances of success on your side.

- Does it make sense for your company to go after this opportunity? Do you have a clear right to play here? Would your people find it obvious that your company should go after such an opportunity? Would your customers see your company playing a role there?

- What existing strengths are you building on? What are the synergies between what you want to do and what you're already doing?

- Does the opportunity help reinforce the role that your company plays in the lives of your customers? Besides the money, is there a compelling reason to go after it?

- Would it be easy to find people who are passionate about pursuing the opportunity? Does it create a sense of excitement? Is it something people would wake up early to work on?

- Is there potential to make a big impact in the world? Can this opportunity allow your company to create a big positive change in the lives of your customers or in their businesses?

When the leadership of a company decides to go after an opportunity, they may neglect how their employees will feel about it. But if you can't get your people to deeply care about pursuing a new opportunity, it'll be difficult to encourage them to give their best for the company to succeed.

Today, there's a hype for "mission-led" or "purpose-led" businesses. Companies embrace sustainability not only because it makes their propositions more desirable, but also because their employees want to feel that their work means something. More and more of us are driven by the "impact" we make in our job.

Optionality

> *"I have never wanted to get an account so big that I could not afford to lose it. The day you do that, you commit yourself to living with fear. Frightened agencies lose the courage to give candid advice; once you lose that you become a lackey."*
>
> – DAVID OGILVY, Advertising Man

Optionality could be seen as a secondary factor. But it remains an important way to manage risks. The more options you have, the less likely you'll end up being stuck in an unwanted situation.

That being said, you must balance optionality with commitment. While it's key to be flexible so you can adapt quickly, you need to put a certain level of focus to make sure that you are truly going after the business opportunity you picked and not just dipping your toes testing lots of different possible routes.

- Are you putting all your eggs in the same basket? If this doesn't work, do you have a possible plan B?

- Are you building assets and capabilities that will be valuable for other projects?

- How long would it take to reallocate your resources? Are you exploring a brand new territory that requires new skills and ways of working? Are you close enough to what you already do so you can quickly repurpose resources?

- How small can you start? Does it require a big upfront investment? Can you gradually commit?

- Will you rely too much on one client or customer? Could you end up in a position where you can't afford to lose your one biggest account?

- Will you be too dependent on one platform or one partner to create and deliver value to your customers?

Some companies make millions of euros by only selling products on Amazon. They benefit from the massive reach of the Amazon marketplace. In 2020, there were 142.5 million Amazon Prime subscribers, and many more millions of customers who buy on Amazon. Besides the enormous visibility that Amazon offers, it's also possible to integrate with Fulfilment by Amazon, a service that offers to pick, pack, ship, and provide customer service for your products.

As a fully-committed Amazon seller, your job is to source the right products and advertise them well on Amazon. Everything else is done for you. Sounds great! Right?

But there's a massive downfall that comes with such a business model… You're at the mercy of Amazon. Every Amazon seller feels that tension. They have to comply with every rule that Amazon creates. They entirely rely on Amazon's algorithms and how they feature products. There are stories of Amazon launching competing products under their own Amazon Basic label. And if Amazon decides to ban a product or a seller for an arbitrary reason, they could see their main stream of revenue fall to 0. This worst-case scenario has happened and will continue to happen.

Being on Amazon may require less upfront investment compared to selling on your own online shop. But it comes at the cost of losing in optionality. If something—which you can't control—happens, your company may suffer a lot.

I'm not saying that committing to Amazon or another platform is a good or bad thing. It depends. And it's a decision that you must consider carefully before making it.

Is it a "product" opportunity or a "feature" opportunity?

> *"In the 1980s, if you installed a word processor or spreadsheet program on your PC, they wouldn't come with word counts, footnotes or charts. Those were all separate products from separate companies that you'd have to go out and buy for $50 or $100 each."*
>
> – BENEDICT EVANS, Independent Analyst

A *"product" opportunity* is the possibility to offer a product or a service to customers who would pay for it and use it to create value that will benefit them or their company.

A *"feature" opportunity* is the possibility to improve an existing product or a service and broaden its scope by adding functionalities that allow it to create more value for the customer or the user.

The question about "product vs. feature" is a lens you can use to evaluate the potential of an opportunity. Note that it can be a matter of perspective, which makes it sometimes difficult to answer the question. There's a grey area that ultimately depends on how the incumbents react to you entering the market.

In my research, I read that Steve Jobs told the founder of Dropbox (launched in 2009) that the company was just building a feature—not a stand-alone product. Indeed… in 2011, Dropbox's success was being threatened when Apple launched iCloud. It was Apple's attempt to "featurise" Dropbox into iOS and macOS by offering a cloud backup feature.

Though Dropbox was highly dependent on Apple's systems, it survived. The Dropbox experience went beyond being the backup feature of an OS, as it also offered cross-OS sharing (e.g., from a MacBook to an Android phone) and file sharing between team members. While iCloud focused on helping you to back up the files that are on your Mac and iPhone, Dropbox was a tool for online collaboration.

Defining whether you're looking at a "product" opportunity or a "feature" opportunity triggers a set of questions across external and internal factors:

- *Desirability* – Does it create enough value for the customers so they get your proposition on top of other products and services?

- *Competitivity* – Could a competitor "swallow" your opportunity by releasing a new feature for their existing product or service? What are the reasons they wouldn't do that?

- *Viability* – Is the potential demand balanced with the cost of creating the product or the service?

- *Optionality* – Do you rely too much on someone else's system to create value for your customers and users?

Sometimes, what seems to be a feature can allow your company to capture material value because the competitor that could release the feature doesn't make it a priority.

In the 2010s, as the growth of podcasting was accelerating, podcast hosts needed tools to record interviews with their guests. The podcasting trend triggered an opportunity to create such a tool. Most podcast hosts at the time had Skype installed on their computers, Ecamm, a software company, saw the opportunity to build a call recorder for Skype. Once the plugin is installed, you can record any Skype call. It's then easy for you to use the audio recording and turn it into a podcast episode.

Ecamm's product seems very much like a feature of Skype. It sounds almost basic that the video conference software would allow you to record calls. But Call Recorder for Skype has existed for a decade or so, and Skype still doesn't have a recording option that suits the needs of podcasters. It's an easy one to fix. But Microsoft may have overlooked the opportunity or considered it was too small to be worth it.

When you think about whether the incumbent could turn

your "product" opportunity into a "feature" opportunity, it's good to explore whether they'll be able to notice the opportunity and whether it'll be big enough for them to believe in it and build it.

Is it a "distribution" opportunity or an "innovation" opportunity?

> *"The battle between every startup and incumbent comes down to whether the startup gets distribution before the incumbent gets innovation."*

– ALEX RAMPELL, General Partner, Andreessen Horowitz

"Distribution vs. innovation" is very much a question of competitivity. Can a new business acquire customers faster than the incumbent can figure out how to make the innovation available to its existing customers?

It works like this: Startups tend to be better at innovating, but they struggle to spread the innovation. Corporates tend to have stronger distribution channels, but they find it hard to commit to creating new products or services.

No matter if you work for a startup or a corporate, you can assess opportunities using this lens: *Is it about creating something new? Or is it about distributing something that seems to be already working?*

In 2011, Dollar Shave Club saw an opportunity to transform how we buy razors. At the time, men complained about how expensive razors are. Michael Dubin, the founder, wondered: "What if we created cheaper razors and sold them using a subscription model?" Instantly, thousands of men fell in love with the proposition. Five years later, Unilever acquired the business for about 1 billion euros.

Whether it was a good idea, only Unilever people know. But what's sure is that the Unilever team that acquired Dollar Shave Club believed that the razor startup had figured out something new that Unilever could help distribute faster. The role of Dollar Shave Club was to discover the innovation. Unilever's role is to scale the distribution.

Pros and cons

> *"Steve [Jobs] stood with [a] marker in hand and scrawled PROS on one side and CONS on the other. [...] Two hours later, the pros were meagre and the cons were abundant, even if a few of them, in my estimation, were quite petty. I felt dispirited. [...] 'A few solid pros are more powerful than dozens of cons,' Steve [Jobs] said. Another lesson: Steve was great at weighing all sides of an issue and not allowing negatives to drown out positives, particularly for things he wanted to accomplish. It was a powerful quality of his."*
>
> – ROBERT IGER, Former CEO, Disney

Pros and cons are this nearly universal decision-making tool. The expression "pros and cons" come from the Latin words "pro" (for) and "contra" (against). It's about assessing the positives and the negatives of a situation to help you make a decision.

Wikipedia calls it a "decisional balance sheet". Some may talk about "upside vs. downside", others use the terms "benefits vs. risks" or "advantages vs. disadvantages".

The key here is not to limit yourself to a listing exercise. While expansive listing is a great way to push you to broaden your range of consideration, it may block you by giving you too many things to pay attention to.

Here are some tips to improve your pros-and-cons list:

1. Only use the most important ones to make an informed decision. You won't go anywhere by trying to consider all the factors of a complex decision. Once you've listed everything, get rid of minor considerations and focus on the most critical items.

2. Take into account the weight of each item. What's misleading on a list is that every item has the same real estate, i.e., a line. Make sure you add a weight parameter. For example, you could qualify the importance on a scale of 0 to 5.

3. Assess the probabilities. Not every pro or con is equally likely to happen, so must make sure to capture the likelihood for each of them. You can add your estimation next to each item or turn your list into a decision tree. If you're not comfortable putting a number on it, you can set the probability as "high", "moderate", or "low".

Pros and cons won't make the decision for you. But listing them, prioritising the most critical ones, and estimating their relative importance and likelihood to happen should help you inform how you decide on the right opportunities to pursue.

The cost of the opportunity

> *"If you take the best text in economics by Mankiw, he says intelligent people make decisions based on opportunity costs—in other words, it's your alternatives that matter. That's how we make all of our decisions."*
>
> – CHARLIE MUNGER,
> Vice Chairman, Berkshire Hathaway

The opportunity cost is a hypothetical cost incurred when you choose one opportunity over all the other available options. When you decide to go for something, you're closing the doors to many other alternatives. This is your opportunity cost.

Charlie Munger and Warren Buffett have a nice way of putting it:

"We just look to do the most intelligent thing we can with the capital that we have. We measure everything against our alternatives."

It often happens that we get excited about an opportunity. Instinctively, our range of choices narrows down to one. This is where the concept of opportunity cost becomes the most important. But it seems that it doesn't come naturally to us. Dan Ariely illustrated it well in a behavioural economics study:

"Money is very difficult to think about. So, we think about money as the opportunity cost of money. So, we at some point went to a Toyota dealership and we asked people, what will you not be able to do in the future if you bought this Toyota? Now, you would expect people to have an answer. But people were kind of shocked by the question."

Indeed, it is important to consider what else could be done with the resources necessary to go after your preferred opportunity. It will help you make sure that other options have been considered and will reinforce your level of confidence that the right opportunity has been chosen.

You can only pick one

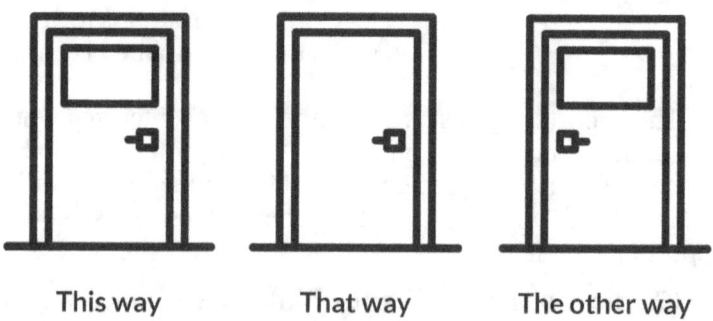

This way   That way   The other way

Investors compute the opportunity cost by looking at the difference between the return on the best-foregone option and the return on the chosen option. But this is different for a business opportunity. Your estimation must go beyond the financial assessment. There are other strategic considerations to take into account such as associated risks and all the other external and internal factors. If something doesn't truly fit with your company's identity, do you still want to pursue the opportunity even if it seems to rank high on viability?

So, here are the questions: *"What must your company give up to choose this or that opportunity?"* *"What else could you do with those resources?"*

Resource allocation

> *"You can talk all you want about having a clear purpose and strategy for your life, but ultimately this means nothing if you are not investing the resources you have in a way that is consistent with your strategy. In the end, a strategy is nothing but good intentions unless it's effectively implemented."*
>
> – CLAYTON CHRISTENSEN, Professor,
> Harvard Business School

Most companies aspire to be ambitious and innovative. But they often say more than they actually do.

The leadership team may say that they want to do things differently. They have a strategy for the future and want to pursue new opportunities. However, it's likely they will commit to a plan to allocate resources that will be, in essence, very similar to what they did the previous years, with only a tiny portion dedicated to the newly stated strategy.

According to a 2012 study by McKinsey that reviewed the performance of 1,600 companies in the US between 1990 and 2005, the wide majority of companies allocated their capital in a similar way to what they did the year before. The mean correlation was about 0.92 across all industries. This shows that most companies get stuck in a form of inertia, following what they did previously rather than truly connecting the resources they allocate to their strategic priorities. The leadership prefers to stay in their comfort zone, making their decisions based on historical data.

The team that led the study noticed that the low-performers were the ones that made only modest shifts in their resource allocation. The top third, which achieved much better returns to shareholders than the bottom third, was able to shift about 50% of their resources year on year. They were more flexible at pursuing new opportunities and committing to do so in the way they allocated relevant resources (e.g., capital, talent, and operating expenditures).

The point I want to make here isn't to give you a magic number based on an old study. It's to push your thinking on two things:

1. If you say that your company is exploring and pursuing new opportunities, how does that translate into numbers?
2. Do you properly challenge your current strategy to make sure that you are allocating enough resources to go after future sources of growth for your company?

In essence, you should "put your money where your strategy is" and "what got you here won't get you there".

Easy opportunity vs. Hard opportunity

> *"The most counterintuitive secret about startups is that it's often easier to succeed with a hard startup than an easy one."*
>
> – SAM ALTMAN, CEO, OpenAI

An *"easy" opportunity* is often the result of a copycat. Someone else has done it before. There are step-by-step instructions to reach what good looks like. You know it won't change the world, but it could be a financially interesting move. It may be new to your company, but it's not new to the world.

A *"hard" opportunity* puts you in front of many challenges. There's real uncertainty as to what needs to be done to succeed. Feasibility is low. Viability may be uncertain. But one thing is sure: the upside is high. The opportunity has game-changing potential. Success would allow your company to create material value for the customers—and possibly for society. Unfortunately, there's no map to guide you. It will be up to you to figure out how to get there.

Whatever opportunity you choose to go after—easy or hard—it will require you to invest time, energy, and resources. But hard opportunities are more inspiring and motivating. They are a powerful vehicle to attract great talent. Your best people don't want to sit for creating a boring replica of something that has been done before. They want to venture into unexplored territory.

Note that your company isn't bound to the dichotomy between "easy" and "hard". Some opportunities sit in between. And there's also the possibility to have a more balanced portfolio of opportunities.

Explore vs. Exploit

> *"Explore when you will have time to use the resulting knowledge, exploit when you're ready to cash in."*
>
> – BRIAN CHRISTIAN, Author

To survive and remain relevant, your company must constantly adapt. What got you here won't get you there. The world never stops changing; so does your company.

But that doesn't mean that your company needs to fully reinvent itself every time the leadership decides to pursue a new business opportunity. Sometimes it does, but most of the time your company must perform a strategic balancing act: exploring new opportunities, while exploiting its current business model.

Exploration is what I have described in this book. It's about broadening the horizon of your company to spot new opportunities and create new sources of revenue.

Exploitation is about getting better at what your company already does. It's about optimising how your company creates and delivers value to your customers by making continuous improvements to existing processes, increasing efficiency, and cutting costs where possible.

Exploring and exploiting can't be both achieved at the same time. These two strategic activities have a radically different relationship to certainty and uncertainty.

If you're part of a team that is set to explore new opportunities, you must be comfortable with uncertainty. Your role is to embrace ambiguity in order to discover new things that your company can do to create and deliver value for your customers. And by doing so, you know that by essence doing news things mean that they might not work.

If you're part of a team whose objective is to exploit an existing business model, you are fighting against ambiguity. Your job is to bring certainty and efficiency to the way the company operates. You work to scale the business and make it safer and more profitable.

At their core exploration and exploitation can't mix. Exploration seeks change and exploitation fights change. But since the exploitative side of the business is the money maker for the next quarter, exploratory capabilities are sometimes seen as a luxury. So you have to push harder for your company to explore, manage uncertainty, and take risks.

Taking risks

> *"There's a tremendous bias against taking risks. Everyone is trying to optimise their ass-covering."*
>
> – ELON MUSK, CEO, SpaceX and Tesla

It's easy to talk about risk-taking, when you're not the one taking the risks. "Easier said than done." But it's an important topic to cover.

Lack of risk-taking is a big contributor to mediocre results. If you don't have ambitious goals, you can't achieve ambitious results. It reminds me of this cheesy metaphor: "Aim for the stars, if you fail, you'll land on the moon." I would add that if you never aim for something in space, you'll never reach anything. But again, "easier said than done."

Let me leave you with two questions here:

1. What results do you expect?
2. Are you sure that you're being ambitious enough?

Your goals or your company's goals are an important lens that you can use to judge what opportunities you and your company want to go after. Being crystal clear on the results that your company expects will help you choose your next business opportunity.

De-risking as you go

> *"Unless you have tested the assumptions in your business model outside the building, your business plan is just creative writing."*
>
> – STEVE BLANK, Adjunct Professor, Stanford University

Being a "risk-taker" shouldn't mean blindly gambling and hoping for the best. Savvy risk-takers don't go all-in from the get-go. They are good at hedging risks. They may start with an ambitious goal, but they gradually commit to taking bigger and bigger risks and learn as they go.

Here's a good example: How do you start an airline when you have no background in running one?

In the 80s, Richard Branson was at the head of a record label and a chain of music shops called Virgin Megastores.

After a bad travel experience, Branson realised that there was an opportunity to compete with the major airlines, which were entrenched in their own ways of doing things. There was apparently so much room to improve the customer experience.

There's quite a big step from running a record label to operating an airline company. Instead of going all-in by buying a fleet of airplanes and serving multiple destinations, Branson started small. Virgin Atlantic began by leasing one secondhand Boeing 747. Had things gone sour, Virgin could have just handed back the plane to Boeing with little costs incurred. Big ambition, low risk.

The way Richard Branson set up Virgin Atlantic demonstrates his approach to managing the risks associated with going after a new opportunity. It's all about containing the risks, and having a timeline at the end of which you decide whether you want to commit and invest more or whether you prefer to pivot or exit the market.

Testing opportunities using ideas

> *"The Googly thing is to launch products early on Google Labs and then iterate, learning what the market wants—and making it great. The beauty of experimenting in this way is that you never get too far from what the market wants. The market pulls you back."*
>
> – MARISSA MAYER, ex-VP, Google

You don't need to lease an airplane to test an opportunity. You can start smaller than that. One way is to make things real by having some potential ideas on how you could go after an opportunity.

At this stage, you shouldn't be precious about these ideas. They're a means to an end, which is why innovation practitioners often call them "sacrificial concepts". They aren't the final answer. Instead, they are a starting point. These ideas are used as a medium for people to react to, so you can collect feedback about whether there's an actual opportunity, as well as insight on how to best go after that opportunity.

Here, you want to test the external and internal factors where you may lack some confidence. If you need to further explore the desirability, you'll show these ideas to potential customers. If it's all about the complexity, you may want to get in touch with potential suppliers and see how they respond to your sacrificial concepts. If you have some doubt about feasibility, you will benefit from presenting these to your internal R&D team or an expert in the field.

Your sacrificial concepts can be brought to life in different formats: an advert (often called an "adcept"), a sales pitch, a leaflet, an app screen, or even just a short description of what you have in mind. You need just enough detail to capture your assumptions and make sure it feels real to the people that should react to your potential ideas.

It's a continuous learning journey

> *"We are all looking for the magic formula. Well, here you go: Creativity + Iterative Development = Innovation."*
>
> – JAMES DYSON, Inventor

Even if you've done extensive research, at the moment when you decide to go after an opportunity, you still have little clue of what's ahead of you. There's no way you can create a 3-year business plan that will correctly predict the course of the next three years.

You and your team will have to continue on your learning journey, getting to know better what works and what doesn't.

Here's a story that illustrates this well.

The team that started Instagram did it after they saw a business opportunity in the smartphone space. In 2009-2010, they were thinking about the fact that soon everyone would have a connected device in their pocket. Remember, the iPhone 3G and the App Store had only launched in 2008.

They realised that these smartphones would allow us to share information in new ways. The team decided to anchor their proposition in geolocation. They created an app whose primary functions were to let users check in to locations, earn points for hanging out with other users, and share pictures with the community.

Very soon after they had started, they got an epiphany. They understood the potential of visual communication. Though photo sharing seemed to be in demand, the users were still shy about sharing their pics. So, the Instagram team found ways to make everyone feel better about posting photos online by giving access to filters. This became a massive hit! While we are less used to relying on filters these days, applying a filter was an essential step for any smartphone photographer in the early 2010s.

There are many stories of "pivot" like this. The team that created Slack, the communication tool, wanted to launch a video game. Twitter should have been a podcasting platform. Before becoming a payment platform, PayPal was originally a way to transfer money via Palm Pilots.

Good judgment

> *"[Judgment] is what enables a sound choice in the absence of clear-cut, relevant data or an obvious path."*
>
> – SIR ANDREW LIKIERMAN, Professor, London Business School

Judgment is your ability to use information and experience in a way that helps you make good decisions when there's some level of uncertainty.

It's both a skill and a way of being. Sir Andrew Likierman summarises it well in a Harvard Business Review article:

> *"I've found that leaders with good judgment tend to be good listeners and readers. They have a breadth of*

experiences and relationships that enable them to recognise parallels or analogies that others miss—and if they don't know something, they'll know someone who does and lean on that person's judgment. They can recognise their own emotions and biases and take them out of the equation. They're adept at expanding the array of choices under consideration. Finally, they remain grounded in the real world: In making a choice they also consider its implementation."

In this dense recipe to exercising good judgment, you can see a few key ingredients:

1. Being open to others' views;
2. Having good sources of information;
3. Building awareness of one's emotions and biases;
4. Encouraging divergent thinking to create multiple options;
5. Adopting a pragmatic approach by having the next steps in mind.

Though judgment is deemed as a personal skill, it's important to get all the elements necessary to exercise good judgment as part of the decision-making process at the organisational level too. Is it the case for your company?

CONCLUSION

In 2018, I wrote The Value Mix to share some useful frameworks that you and your company business can use to create meaningful products and services for your customers. The book aimed to equip the readers with the tools that would help them understand better what their customers want, as well as translate their insight into a compelling product strategy.

There was a gap in how the most used innovation processes (e.g., design thinking, customer development, and the lean startup) spoke about value creation. Innovation is often reduced to identifying problems and solving them. My goal with The Value Mix was to build upon these processes by giving some tools that expand the realm of value creation.

With The Opportunity Lenses, I wanted to take a step back on how businesses innovate… I saw another gap in the management and business literature.

We're all obsessed with ideas. "I want to start my own business, but I don't have a good idea yet." But there's something important that comes before having ideas: the opportunity. Is there an opportunity here? And is this opportunity good for you?

Spotting opportunities requires you to look at the world differently. It's about learning how to see. And when it's hard to see something, you need to put the right lenses on.

My hope is that sharing the lenses will help you unlock new paths for your company or the companies of your clients.

Spotting business opportunities is a never-ending game. Things will continue to change. Some opportunities will die. New opportunities will arise. Put the right lenses on. Explore the world. And build the next big businesses that will positively impact our world.

Book 2

THE
VALUE MIX

THE FRAMEWORK TO CREATE
MEANINGFUL PRODUCTS AND
SERVICES FOR
YOUR AUDIENCE

Introduction

It's difficult to create a product that people really want to buy and use. There's no silver bullet to success. It's hard work because there's lots of uncertainty.

Those who do this for a living know that.

Fortunately, over the past two decades, the management literature has equipped us with better ways to create new products, such as:

1. **Customer centricity.** *Design thinking* and *customer development* are two approaches that encourage us to build products for potential customers rather than trying to find customers for new products;
2. **Iterative development.** The *lean startup* methodology pushes us to apply the scientific method and pursue continuous learning and product iteration to create better products.

But, we are still missing a way to organise the information and insight we gather about our customers to clearly define what they need and want.

To help you develop successful products and services, you need a framework that:

1. Allows you to gain a deep understanding of what value means for your customers;
2. Gives you a shared language to align with your team on a strategy for the new products and services that you will launch.

This framework must be as accurate as possible, by capturing enough nuances to reflect the reality of our world.

But it also needs to be practical enough so it can be used by anyone in your company who is involved in the process of launching new products and services.

Going beyond a limiting framework

Under the pressure of growth and profit targets, most organisations focus too much on their commercial priorities and not enough on creating value for their customers and users.

Putting the people who buy and use your products and services at the centre of your new product development process sounds common sense. But this isn't an intuitive behaviour. It seems that it's easier for a company to be product-centric than human-centred.

The easy way to force a business to focus on their customers and users is to talk about "finding a solution to a problem", i.e., your customers have *problems* and your product is the *solution*.

This framework, which comes from the world of engineering, does help. But it creates the limiting belief that innovation is about "finding a solution to a problem". The "problem-solution" dichotomy works. But it doesn't capture enough nuances. This framework limits the scope of value creation. It misses the fact that people do not just buy a solution. They also buy brands, stories, emotional benefits, and experiences.

Solving a problem isn't the only way to create value for your customers. What people perceive as value isn't just functional. It also relies on how your products and services make them feel.

Innocent, a smoothie brand, didn't create value for its customers by solving a "smoothie" problem. The company created stories and remarkable experiences that made people feel connected to the Innocent brand.

Marshall, a brand known for its music amplifiers, didn't solve a "headphones" problem when it launched a range of branded headphones. The brand built on its heritage of music amplifiers, creating value by making its customers dream and feel like they were at a concert watching their favourite band.

How to make the most of reading these pages

> *"Action is what produces results. Knowledge is only potential power until it comes into the hands of someone who knows how to get himself to take effective action."*
>
> – *TONY ROBBINS, Life strategist*

The Value Mix aims to make it easier for you to think about the nuances of creating products and services that people will want, i.e., creating value for them.

I wanted this framework to be simple to remember and easy to use, while still acknowledging the complexity and nuances of the real world.

Together, we will go through each element of the Value Mix. You'll get everything you need to understand the concept of value creation and then turn what you learnt into action.

Let me emphasise that this isn't a box-filling exercise.

Reality is complex. So, one cannot pretend to capture in a single framework all the nuances necessary to create successful products and services.

This book aims to guide your thinking. The real value lies in doing the work, i.e., understanding your customers at a deeper emotional level and developing new ways to create value for them.

I would call it a success if the Value Mix inspires you to approach more effectively how you research your market and how you build new products and services.

The ultimate objective: creating value for your customers by building the products and services that matter to them.

The inception of the Value Mix

> *"Creativity is just connecting things. When you ask creative people how they did something, they feel a little guilty because they didn't really do it, they just saw something."*
>
> – *STEVE JOBS, Founder of Apple*

New ideas come from finding connections among the things we've experienced, heard, read, and observed.

This is how I got the idea for the Value Mix.

The ideas in this book come from connecting many things: my journey building my own businesses, my experience running innovation projects for Fortune 500 companies, chats with fellow entrepreneurs and investors, and the writing of many businesspeople.

These ideas also connect multiple disciplines, such as economics, design, psychology, copywriting, strategy, software development, and marketing.

The result:

We are lucky as we live in an ocean of nearly free information. The difficulty is to make this knowledge practical so it can help us be more creative and make better decisions.

The value of this book comes from turning the elements related to creating new products and services into a logical framework. It will help you as you build a new business, innovate in an established organisation, or invest in startups.

PART ONE

Creating Value

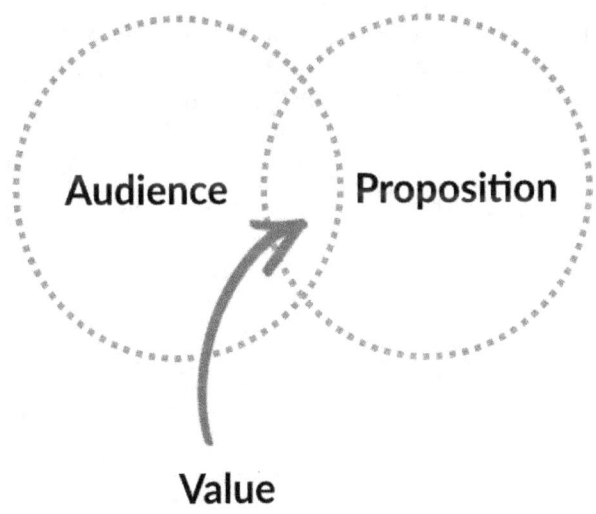

The imperative of value creation

> *"The value is in what gets used, not in what gets built."*
>
> – KRIS GALE, *Founder of Clover Health*

Your business can only succeed if it creates and sells products and services that your audience will want to buy and use—a meaningful proposition.

What's clear is that your audience will want what you sell only if they believe that it creates for them more value than something else, they could buy and use.

So how do you make sure you create value? What are the elements that can help you understand your audience? And what are the things you need to consider to create the right proposition?

Audience: Those you serve

The left side of the framework represents the **audience**, i.e., the people who will buy and use your products and services.

It includes three elements that help you segment your market by answering the following questions:

> What are their beliefs?
> What are they trying to achieve?
> What would prevent them from choosing your proposition?

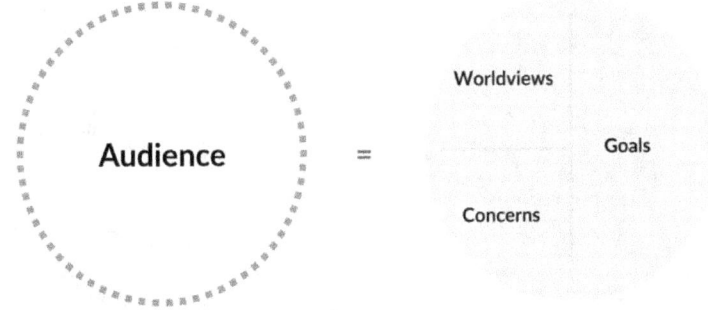

This side of the framework aims to help you identify what creates value for your audience.

Proposition: What you offer

The right side of the Value Mix framework is about your proposition, i.e., what you offer to create value in the lives of your customers and users.

There are a number of elements you can play with to design a proposition that feels meaningful and relevant.

It's is not just about the functionalities of a product or a service. It's about the overall experience you create for your audience.

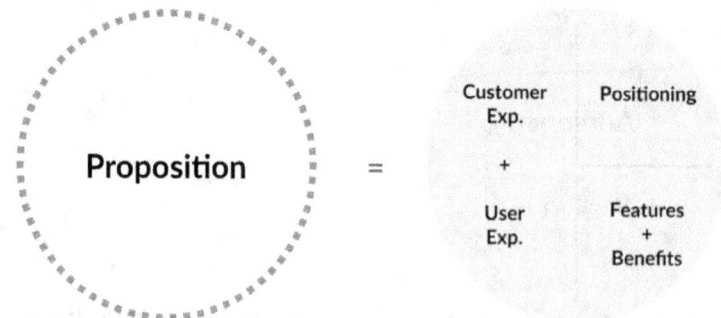

As a proposition, the iPhone isn't just a high-end smartphone. It's also about how you experience the interoperability with the AppStore, the AirPods, iCloud, Apple TV, Safari, Apple Wallet, and the MacBook.

Landscape: When your audience and proposition interact

Your **audience** and your **proposition** do not live in a vacuum. In the real world:

> Your audience lives in a specific **context**. They are in an environment and experience situations that influence what they do and how they think.
>
> Your proposition is constantly compared to **alternatives**. When someone in your target audience considers buying your product, they often have a set of other alternatives in mind.

Having clarity on the context of your audience's life and the set of alternatives that are available to them is decisive in creating a proposition that is relevant and meaningful for your audience.

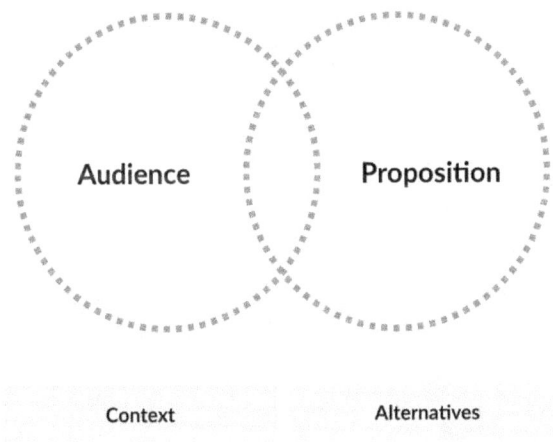

PART TWO

Understanding Your Audience

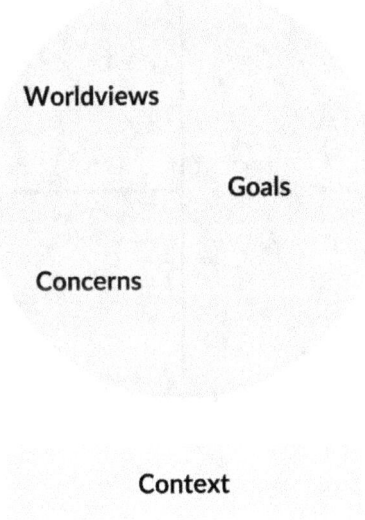

CHAPTER ONE:

Your Audience

"The purpose of business is to create and keep a customer."

– PETER DRUCKER, *Management consultant*

To create meaningful propositions, you must understand what can create value for your audience. You have to be clear on why they need you in their lives.

Leading brands are *audience-informed* (2) but they are *vision-led* (1).

1. It's your role to set the vision and create propositions that your audience will want but never think to ask.
2. But to create something they want, you need to understand your market. You need to have clear answers to: Who is it for? Why will they get it?

As you try to understand your audience at a deeper level to identify what they need and want, there are four things that you should especially focus on:

> **Context** - The context is the surrounding that influences what your audience needs and wants to achieve—their goals.
> **Goals** - In the pursuit of goals, your audience will buy and use products and services that help them achieve the progress and outcomes they envision.
> **Worldviews** - To choose which products and services to buy and use, they rely on their worldviews, which are

the beliefs, biases, and opinions they hold about the world.

Concerns - They also interrogate their concerns about what they are about to buy. These are all the reasons and feelings that are holding them back from buying your proposition (or an alternative one).

CHAPTER TWO:

Context

They know what you need

A few years ago, I visited Milan over the summer. There were a lot of hawkers selling things in the street.

Here's what I noticed:

On a beautiful sunny day, they would sell sunglasses and cold water. But if it started raining, you would see them immediately selling umbrellas and waterproof ponchos.

These street hawkers understood how context influences what people want.

Context: Definition

Context includes time, location, situations, people, weather, events, and all the surrounding that trigger the need or desire to achieve a goal.

Context is a **link of causality**. It causes someone to want to do something. Knowing what the **triggers** are will help you to identify what your audience needs or wants to achieve and why.

For example, a nutritionist must understand the events and situations that trigger a need or desire to change one's diet. Is it a New Year's resolution? Is it because of a wedding? Is it related to a health issue? Knowing the context will help the nutritionist reach her clients at the right time and offer the right approach.

Correlation is not causality

It's Thursday night. Here's Jake, a 27-year-old who works as a senior designer for a tech company in New York.

Can you guess what happens next? Probably not…

Knowing that Jake is a male who is 27 and works in design for a tech company doesn't tell us why on a Thursday night he got takeaway pizzas and why on another night he went to a trendy cocktail bar.

Attributes don't tell us much about what people do. They may correlate with some behaviours. But they do not cause them.

Context is the trigger. It gives you more insight into what people want to achieve.

Maybe Jake got pizzas because he had friends coming over to play poker. The context of playing poker with his friends triggered the desire and need to get some food. As its convenient, cheap, and yummy, pizzas seemed a good option.

A tool: Why create a customer journey

To understand the context your audience lives in, you have to put yourself in their shoes.

> What is the context of the purchase?
> What has triggered their decision?
> And what is the context of use?

Building a **customer journey** helps gain clarity on all the steps that led someone to buy a product or service and to use it.

It is a great tool to create a proposition that truly helps your audience achieve their goals. But it's also helpful to define how, when, and where your proposition must show up in their lives.

A customer journey is a **visual guide**—not the truth. It helps visualise what is happening in the real world. The complexity and variety of customer journeys cannot be modelled accurately.

That being said, even a rough customer journey will help you understand your audience at a deeper level.

By mapping the customer journeys of your audience, you will better understand what triggers specific needs and desires. It will help you create more relevant propositions, and also allow you to identify the best moment and channels to reach them.

Think again about the example of the nutritionist. If the nutritionist understands that most brides start thinking about a new diet when they try wedding dresses, she could partner with brands to offer tailored nutrition plan for the future brides and advertise them in stores, in wedding magazines, and on Pinterest by targeting keywords related to getting married.

A tool: How to create a customer journey

First, choose who in your audience you want to focus on.

Then, map the key moments of the journey. An easy way to start is to use the five following steps: (1) Awareness, (2) Consideration, (3) Purchase, (4) Use (or Consumption), and (5) Referral.

To build the journey, you pick two steps and you ask yourself: "What happens in between?". And you keep doing this—picking two steps and breaking down what happens in between—until you get to a satisfying level of nuance and granularity.

For each step, you must find out what your audience is doing (*actions*), struggling with (*frustrations*), and wishing (*aspirations*).

Depending on your level of knowledge of your audience, you may need to do additional research to have a clearer view of what happens at each step.

Stage	Aware	Consider	Purchase	Use	Refer
Doing					
Struggling with					
Wishing					

Example format for a customer journey

Key questions about your audience

Here are some questions that can guide the way you generate customer insight:

When your audience is in a particular context:

What are they trying to achieve (*goals*)?

What are the beliefs that influence what they're trying to do (*worldviews*)?

What could prevent them from doing this with your proposition (*concerns*)?

Let's now dig into each question.

CHAPTER THREE:

Goals

A new job. But why?

Miranda (not her real name) was working as a cashier in a supermarket. She liked the company but her schedule didn't suit her family life. She would be off when her son was in school and would often have to work quite late in the evening.

But recently, one of her friends started working as a software developer for a startup. It pays well, apparently. So, Miranda saw coding as an opportunity to get a better job. She wanted to be there for her family.

Miranda started using Codecademy, a learning platform. She would study and do the exercises before and after work, even during her lunch breaks to finish the course so that she could move out of retail and do something interesting that would suit better her family life.

Let's dig into the details:

Here Miranda wasn't pleased with her current job because the schedule didn't suit her family life (*context*).

She decided that she'd like to get a job as a developer to be able to spend more time with her family (*goal*).

So, she started taking online classes on Codecademy (*proposition*) to learn about coding and get a job she will like more (*achieved goal*).

Goals: Definition

> *"People don't want to buy a quarter-inch drill. They want a quarter-inch hole!"*
>
> – *THEODORE LEVITT, Professor at Harvard Business School*

A **goal** is the outcome or progress your target audience needs or wants to achieve in a particular context.

Context and goals go together.

The context triggers the goals that lead to buying and using a product or a service.

Focusing on the goals of your target audience helps you spot what causes them to buy and use your proposition or an alternative one.

When the owner of a small e-commerce website is planning the marketing strategy of her business (*context*), she wants to be able to analyse the performance of previous marketing campaigns (*goal*). This causes her to use Google Analytics (*proposition*).

Here are two ways to link context and goals together:

When … (*context*), I want to … (*goal*) by using … (*proposition*).

Here is where I am today (*current context*). And here is where I want your product or service (*proposition*) to take me (*achieved goal*).

What to do with this: Segment the market accurately

> *"Your most unhappy customers are your greatest source of learning."*
>
> — BILL GATES, *ex-CEO of Microsoft*

You can use goals to identify different segments in the market. Once you know precisely what they want to achieve, you can create propositions that are more relevant in the way they help each segment.

Most of the time, a proposition didn't satisfy a customer because it didn't help them achieve their goals. It didn't match their expectations.

For example, someone in Ireland buys a nice coat for the mid-season. But it happens that the coat is just water-resistant, it's not fully waterproof. So, after a heavy rain, the customer is disappointed. He thought he had a nice coat for commuting to work. Now, he realised he can't wear it when it rains.

Identifying the specific goals of each segment will help you make sure that you can address their needs and desires in the most relevant ways, and articulate well how you position your proposition.

Goal-based segmentation often shows up in the pricing strategy of a business.

Airlines master the art of goal-based segmentation, even giving names to the different tiers based on what the segment of the audience is trying to achieve:

> Economy class is designed for those who want to go from A to B as cheaply as possible.
>
> Business class is designed for those who are going from A to B and want to be in the right conditions to be able to work before, during, and after the flight.

What to do with this: Build the right proposition

> *"The customer rarely buys what the business thinks it sells him."*
>
> – PETER DRUCKER, *Management consultant*

Helping your audience achieve their goals in the most effective and efficient way is at the core of creating value for them.

So being clear on the goals of your target audience makes a big difference. Once you really understand what they want to achieve, it makes building the right proposition so much easier, because you now know what to focus on.

Spotify transformed the way we listen to music. Its product team has been focused on helping users achieve their goals around listening to music, making the experience so much better than buying and using CDs. For that, the company created new features such as:

- A Friend feed (*feature*), when you want to share the music you like with your friends and what music they listen to (*goal*);
- Sport playlists (*feature*), when you want to motivate yourself with some music when you go running (*goal*);
- Spotify Discover (*feature*), when you need new ideas of music to listen to (*goal*).

Goals are the foundation on which you can build the features and customer experience that will be most helpful to your audience.

What to do with this: Find new opportunities

"People don't like to be sold but they love to buy."

– JEFFREY GITOMER, Sales consultant

When we define the goals of an audience, it's tempting to focus more on the functional aspect of their goals, e.g., "When I travel for work, I need to have a small suitcase that is allowed in the cabin".

A company that identifies that goal will inevitably have a narrow focus on selling suitcases that can be accepted in the cabin.

But if you dig deeper into the emotional aspect by asking "why?", you may realise that it may be about the speed of boarding, but it's also about safety, i.e., "When I travel for work, I need a small suitcase that guarantees that I can have with me in the cabin, because I want to know that my stuff is safe."

Here's the interesting insight coming out!

The second expression of the goal allows many more possibilities to help your audience. Now, it's not just about making a compact suitcase. It's also about making a suitcase that will reassure them that no one will be able to open it. You want to make your audience feel that when they put their belongings in the suitcase, it's almost as safe as putting them in a safe deposit box.

By reframing the goals and really digging into the emotional aspect, you may uncover interesting insight that will spark new ideas on how you can best serve your audience.

A tool: Customer interviews

As you saw in the example above, interviewing your customers can help you uncover useful bits of insight that will then allow you to create more value for them.

But for this, you need to ask good questions.

You should avoid asking conditional questions using "would". These lead to vague or generic answers about what someone would do in a hypothetical situation.

Instead, ask for stories. Ask questions about what someone did in the past.

Try to get as much detail as possible to really understand what they did and how they felt. And then, politely dig into the reasons they did these things, or felt that way by asking them "why?". Don't hesitate to ask "why?" several times. You often get the best insight after the second or third "why".

Here's an example about going to the gym: When I ask someone: "Do you go to the gym?" They often tell me: "Yes. I go 3-4 times a week." But then, if I ask: "What about last week? Did you go to the gym?" The usual answer is: "Hmmm. No. But that's different. I didn't go because…"

A generic claim isn't as good as a specific story.

Bad questions are generic or conditional: Do you ever do…? Do you think you would…? If [conditional event], would you…?

Better questions are specific and about the past: What did you do? When did you…? Where? With whom? Why did you decide to do this? How did you feel? Tell me more about that. Why did you feel that way?

A key question about your audience:

What goals are you helping your audience to achieve?

CHAPTER FOUR:

Worldviews

What makes them cool?

When the summer comes (*context*), we start wearing sunglasses to protect our eyes (*functional goal*) and look cool (*emotional goal*).

This is the case for Peter and Alex who both live in Paris. Both of them have similar goals when it gets sunny: "to protect their eyes and to look cool".

But then, how can we explain that Peter wears a classic pair of Ray-Ban, while Alex has a pair, he bought from a startup brand called Jimmy Fairly?

They aren't interested in the same stories.

Let's dig into the details:

Peter and Alex share similar goals. But they have different worldviews, i.e., different sets of values, beliefs, biases, and opinions.

They both relied (unconsciously) on their own worldviews to guide their choice of sunglasses.

> Peter felt reassured about Ray-Ban. It's a well-known brand and most people would approve his choice.
> Alex wanted something more social and less mainstream. He values that Jimmy Fairly gives a pair of glasses to someone in need when he buys his own pair of stylish

glasses. And he likes that not that many people actually know about the brand.

Worldviews: Definition

> *"A worldview is not who you are. It's what you believe. It's your biases. A worldview is not forever. It's what the consumer believes right now."*
>
> – SETH GODIN, *Author of All Marketers Are Liars*

The context tells you why and when some specific goals arise in your customers' lives. And the goals tell you what they are trying to achieve. But context and goals cannot tell us why someone chooses a brand over another one.

This is what worldviews help you do.

Worldviews are a set of beliefs, values, taste, attitudes, and opinions that your audience relies on when they make decisions.

A worldview is subjective. It's a personal preference that is based on what someone believes to be true.

You can think of worldviews as a way of seeing and judging things. They are the lenses through which your audience looks at the world when they are trying to achieve their goals. Worldviews guide your audience's actions and influence their choices.

Why does someone decide to buy a $450 Dyson vacuum cleaner, while someone else goes for a Eureka vacuum cleaner, which is labelled as the Amazon's First Choice and costs only $69?

Maybe it's a difference in disposable income. Or maybe it's that the former customer loves well-designed products, and the latter believes it's good to be frugal.

Dyson tells the "design" story well. And Eureka positioned itself to speak the language of frugality showing good value for money.

What to do with this: A segmentation tool

"Segments must be Measurable, Substantial, Accessible, Differentiable, and Actionable."

— PHILIP KOTLER, *Professor at the Kellogg School of Management*

Worldviews are useful criteria for **segmenting** your market. What people believe to be true can help you predict their decisions more accurately than their age or their job.

Looking at worldviews gives you the nuances that you miss when you only search for "customer problems". It tells you at a deeper level why someone chooses an alternative versus another.

Young parents face many challenges. On the weekend (*context*), one of their problems is: "How can we have a nice family time and make our children happy?" (*goal*).

For some parents, McDonald's means Happy Meal, Big Mac, nostalgia, and nice moments with their children (*worldview*). For other parents, McDonald's means junk food, saturated fat, and too much carb. It's something they don't want their children to have (*worldview*).

Of course, this is a simplified view of the market. But here's the question: If you were running McDonald's, would you try to please both worldviews?

What to do with this: A storytelling tool

"Great brands are the ones that tell the best stories. Sure, good products and service matter, but stories are what connect people with companies."

— *JASON FRIED, CEO of Basecamp*

Telling stories is key to building a strong brand. Stories are what make a product stand out in front of your audience. Meaningful propositions don't just solve a functional problem; they create an emotional connection between your brand and your audience.

Stories help you affirm why your product or service exists. It tells your customers how your proposition creates.

A common model of story is the "before and after" story. Describe their lives before your proposition was part of their day-to-day. Then, tell the story of how your proposition can transform their lives and what outcome it can help them achieve.

If you want to get someone excited about signing up for your upcoming online course, you don't spend hours explaining the outline of the course. You tell them about how this course can transform their personal or professional lives, i.e., what value it creates for them. A compelling way to do so is to tell them the story of their lives after they've taken the course.

The ad of an online course about yoga may tell you about how you will never have your terrible back pain anymore or how a daily yoga session will keep you energised throughout the day.

Good stories reinforce the existing worldviews of your audience. They don't try to get them to change their mind.

In the example above, the yoga course reinforces the belief that having the right level of physical activity can help alleviate back pain or make you feel more energetic.

Ways of telling stories

Storytelling is not just about copywriting and advertising.

The smell of a French bakery tells the story of "fresh bread". The cocktail offered at a nail salon tells the story of "pampering".

You build a story through every aspect of the customer experience.

In 2011, I created GoudronBlanc, a brand that makes elegant T-shirts that men love. A worldview I spotted was that more and more men wear T-shirts instead of suits when they are at work.

To tell the story of what I call "T-shirt is the new suit", I took photos of famous French entrepreneurs wearing GoudronBlanc T-shirts in their office. The story was even covered by a national newspaper.

As said before, a good story is anchored in existing beliefs. It confirms your audience's biases. It plays on their perception.

But the story has to be true. If your proposition cannot deliver on what you're promising, it won't work.

Evaluating worldviews

> *"Marketing succeeds when enough people with similar worldviews come together in a way that allows marketers to reach them cost-effectively."*
>
> – SETH GODIN, *Author of All Marketers Are Liars*

Now, you understand how worldviews play a significant role in how your audience assesses value and makes choices.

Worldviews are subjective. They are based on personal experiences, on what others say, on how the world reacts to what one does.

Most worldviews are personal. But some worldviews are shared.

To build successful propositions, you want to address worldviews that are shared by a group of people. When people have a common worldview, they talk about it. They talk about the products and services that relate to that worldview.

And this will make it easier for your ideas and stories to spread at an affordable cost, through word of mouth.

Professionals who value their time highly will always be keen on telling others about their productivity system. If there's a new app they find exciting, they will blog about it, share it on social media, and may even share YouTube videos about how to use it.

Chocolate lovers, who believe that industrial chocolate isn't worth a penny, will be super enthusiastic with the idea of telling their friends about a new artisanal chocolate brand.

How to spot worldviews

Identifying worldviews is about spotting patterns. It's the difficult work of the innovator, the market researcher, the product manager, or the investor.

There isn't a magic way of doing it. But some things can help you find evidence that a worldview exists:

- **Social Listening:** Browse forums, Reddit, Facebook groups, YouTube videos, blog articles. What are some of the most viral articles and videos? What do people tell each other on social media?
- **Customer Interviews:** Interview people who share a hobby, have similar lifestyles, etc. What do they believe strongly? Have they recently started doing something new?

When doing social listening and customer interviews, it's worth paying extra attention to a few things, such as:

- **Influencers** — Who are the people who seem to lead and spread the worldview?
- **Books they read** — What are the books they read and recommend?
- **Videos they watch** — What are the movies, documentaries, and YouTube videos they watch and recommend?
- **Places they go to** — Where can you find them? Are there specific online platforms where they hang out?
- **Brands they use** — What are other brands they buy and talk about? Why these?

Example: The digital nomad worldview

Who they are:

Digital nomads are a community of people who work remotely to live nomadic lives. They often take advantage of not having to be in an office to travel and live in foreign countries.

The evidence they exist:
- **What they read:** 4-Hour Workweek, Vagabonding
- **Influencers:** Matt Mullenweg, Tim Ferriss

Where they hang out: nomadlist.com, reddit.com/r/digitalnomad/, coworking spaces, coffee shops…

Brands they use: Cocoon (cable organiser), Qwstion (backpack), Revolut (banking)

What they say and believe:

"I'm young. Why should I be trapped in a life that isn't for me?"

"The corporate world is boring."

"If I can do it remotely, why should I commute to an office?"

"Have you been in Asia? There are so many cool things to explore."

"Why should I live in an expensive American city, when I can have a much better life abroad?"

A key question about your audience:

What shared worldviews are you addressing?

CHAPTER FIVE:

Concerns

In search of the perfect travel companion

I have some back issues. This can turn a long-haul flight into a nightmare.

In April 2018, I had 5 long haul flights booked to travel for work and leisure (*context*). As I wanted to avoid suffering from lower back pain while travelling (*goal*), I started searching for the perfect travel pillow (*proposition*).

After a few Google searches, I short-listed five brands. All seemed to do the job. But then, I started asking myself:

> Is it going to be firm enough to hold my head?
> Is the pillow going to lose its shape if I fold it into my bag?
> What about the fabric, is it going to be comfortable or make my skin itchy?

All of these questions are concerns.

They can be dangerous for a brand, as they can stop a prospect from buying.

The brand that ultimately won my purchase is the one that created the most certainty. It answered all of my questions and reassured me that I was buying a good travel pillow.

Concerns: Definition

> *"There is only one boss. The customer. And he can fire everybody in the company from the chairman on down, simply by spending his money somewhere else."*
>
> — *SAM WALTON, Founder of Walmart*

Concerns are all the arguments (*logical reasons*) and feelings (*emotional reasons*) that prevent your target customers from buying your proposition or an alternative one.

When we think about concerns, we often consider "price" first.

But concerns are not just about price-sensitivity. They also include the "learning curve", "switching cost", lack of social proof, lack of clarity on how it works, the pricing model, questions about durability, or a new version of your product that is coming soon.

The level of concerns depends on the context and what your audience wants to achieve.

The concerns about buying a new smartphone are more important than the concerns about trying a new brand of Greek yoghurt.

In B to B, the concerns about contracting for a new cloud service are more significant than the concerns about choosing the food provider for a company event. This will often translate into the number of people involved in making the decision.

It's always a "logical" concern

The concerns of your audience come from the potential negative consequences that they want to avoid when they buy and use your proposition.

> I ordered this new flavoured tea, but I don't like the taste.
> I bought these shoes online, but they don't fit me.
> I subscribed to a fashion magazine, but the content isn't as good as I expected.
> I signed up to a CRM tool, but there are lots of hidden costs.

These are all "logical" stories that your potential customers are telling themselves. Some may be objective; others may be more subjective.

I put logical in quotation marks to emphasise the following point: these stories are logical to them. You may think: "It's crazy to worry about this". But what matters is what's in their minds, not what's in yours.

Anticipating concerns when you create your proposition makes it easier to sell it later. It's about designing the customer experience to answer the questions from the voice that is in the head of your audience.

You want your proposition to reassure them that they are making the right decision.

Certainty plays a big role

When you sell a product or a service, you sell *certainty*.

You sell:

> the certainty that it's the best offer available,
> the certainty that they are making the right decision,
> the certainty that it's going to work as they expect,
> the certainty that their friends will like it,
> the certainty that the boss will be happy, etc.

Concerns arise when your audience feels that there's a lack of certainty.

This is why good marketers focus on building trust with their target audience. The more trustworthy you appear, the easier it is for your audience to buy.

Free trial, freemium, referral, affiliate, user-generated content, etc. These are many features you can bake into the customer experience to increase certainty (and reduce concerns) when your audience is considering buying your proposition.

> A key question about your audience:
>
> What will hold people back from buying your proposition?

PART THREE

Shaping Your Proposition

Audience
= your prospects and customers

Proposition
= your product or service

Worldviews

Goals

Concerns

Customer Exp.

Positioning

+

User Exp.

Features
+
Benefits

Context

Alternatives

CHAPTER SIX:

Your proposition

"Ideas don't come out fully formed. They only become clear as you work on them. You just have to get started."

— *MARK ZUCKERBERG, CEO of Facebook*

It's quite easy to come up with new product ideas. A typical ideation workshop can lead to a hundred or more ideas.

What's more difficult is to turn these ideas into fully-fledged propositions.

The lack of detail about a proposition can become a barrier to implementing it. You need to be clear on the detail to align with your team. You must be able to articulate your proposition to make a business case for investing in testing it and implementing it.

You need clarity on the detail to be able to test your proposition with potential customers by following the *lean startup* or *design thinking* methodology.

The **proposition** comes after the audience in the book because a proposition is something you build *for* an audience. It's about making something for your audience, instead of trying to find customers for what you made.

To create value for your audience, you must understand them first. Then, once you understand the context, their goals, their worldviews, and their concerns, it'll be easier to create propositions that are right for them.

In this section, I explore the six elements that you must consider to build a coherent proposition. The objective is to give you and your team a shared language to work on creating meaningful propositions.

I'll focus on the following:

> **Alternatives** – Alternatives are the benchmarks you can use to make sure you build a relevant proposition.
> **Features and Benefits** – While benefits are about helping your audience achieve their goals, features help you describe and prioritise what needs to be built.
> **Positioning** – Your positioning is how you'd like your audience to perceive your proposition and what you want them to remember and tell their friends about it.
> **CX and UX** – The customer experience (CX) and user experience (UX) are the ways your proposition shows up in the lives of your customers (and users).

CHAPTER SEVEN:

Alternatives

The best way to travel

When I was studying in London, the holiday period (*context*) was the perfect moment to go to Paris to visit my parents (*goal*).

I had several options: train, coach, airplane, or getting someone to drive me there.

As a student, I had time but no money (*worldview*), so the Eurostar, the fastest way to get there, wasn't my only alternative.

Every time I would go to Paris, I was balancing price, comfort, and the speed to choose how to get there.

Eurostar is a railway service. Ouibus, Eurolines, and Megabus are in the bus industry. Air France and Ryan Air are airlines. BlaBlaCar is in an online marketplace.

But every time I wanted to go to Paris, they were all competing for my pennies.

They are all alternatives to one another.

Alternatives: Definition

Alternatives are propositions that your audience perceives as comparable, since they can also help them achieve their goals.

Once they bought an alternative, they become less interested in having the other alternative propositions. It's what economists call the "law of diminishing marginal utility". If you just bought a new smartphone, you're less interested in having another one.

Businesses usually look at competitive propositions in their category, i.e., direct competitors.

But it is more accurate to look at the competitive landscape from the eyes of your audience, comparing goal-based alternatives.

Example:

Who is the biggest competitor of Coca-Cola (the soda)?

> Pepsi? Red Bull?
> Fruit juices? Smoothies?
> Wine? Beer?
> Coffee? Tea?
> Water?

Unintended consequences

> *"The reason [the railroads] defined their industry incorrectly was that they were railroad oriented instead of transportation oriented. They were product-oriented instead of customer-oriented."*
>
> – THEODORE LEVITT, *Professor at Harvard Business School*

The issue with only considering direct competitors instead of a broader set of alternatives is that a company may tend to focus on the features of its proposition, not on what its audience is trying to achieve.

The company ends up in an arms race trying to offer better features and functionalities than its direct competitors. But they miss the point because they are not looking at the world in the way their audience does.

The direct competitor of a DSLR camera is another DSLR camera. But when someone wants to take photos, they may also consider other alternatives such as a smartphone, a disposable camera, a Polaroid, or a GoPro. That's because they are looking for the best way to achieve their goals, which also fits with their worldview. They are not limiting themselves to a product category.

It's important to look at your market from the point of view of your audience.

Knowing what your audience considers as alternatives gives useful information on their goals, their worldviews, and therefore what's important for them when they make their choice.

It's a good source of insight to build a more relevant proposition. It gives you the material to build a story and position your proposition in a way that speaks to your audience and makes it stand out against the other alternatives.

A tool: Alternatives mapping

An **alternatives map** is a tool that helps visualise how your audience thinks about your proposition compared to relevant alternatives.

It helps you gain clarity on their decision-making process:

> What criteria matter to them?
> How do alternatives compare to each other?
> What alternative performs the best?

Understanding how your audience chooses the best option for them will help you better design a proposition that will create more value for them.

Here are the steps necessary to build an alternatives map:

1. Identify the range of alternatives that your audience is likely to compare with one another;
2. Lay out the criteria they use to make their decisions of buying one over another;
3. Rank how each alternative performs for each criterion.

Here's an example of an alternatives map for someone who wants to go from London to Paris:

Alternatives for going from London to Paris

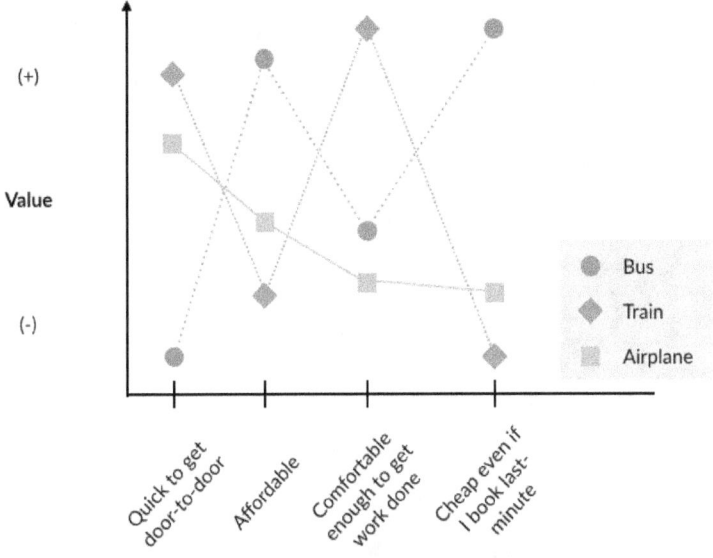

Attributes that matter to your audience

It's clear that the train is the fastest and most comfortable alternative. Going by bus is the most affordable and flexible option. Flying to Paris is somewhat in between.

A key question about your proposition:

What alternatives does your target audience have in mind when they consider your proposition?

CHAPTER EIGHT:

Feature + Benefits

The one who wanted to show off

I'll never forget this scene from Friends:

Chandler opens a bulky laptop, which is typical of the 90s, and says: "All right! Check out this bad boy."

Describing his new computer with pride, he adds: "12 Megabytes of RAM. 500-megabyte hard drive. Built-in spreadsheet capabilities... And a modem that transmits at over 28,000 BPS."

Unimpressed, Phoebe comments asking: "What are you gonna use it for?"

Chandler looks a bit confused and replies saying: "Games and stuff..."

Let's decode what happened here:

The scene is turning into ridicule the fact that features are simply the characteristics of a proposition. Being proud of features doesn't make sense.

And this is what makes the scene funny: A mere list of feature misses the "so what?", which is what Phoebe is asking with a candid tone. "What are you gonna use it for?"

Features do not tell you what a proposition is for. They don't say anything about how people will use it and how it creates value for them.

Features are useful to build a proposition. But your audience will find the benefits to be more relevant.

Feature: Definition

> *"Roadmaps are evidence of strategy. Not a list of features."*
>
> – STEVE JOHNSON, *Product management expert*

Features help you describe your proposition at a technical level. They are all the characteristics and functionalities of your proposition.

Also called specs, features are especially useful in two situations:

1. Comparing propositions – By breaking down your proposition into individual features, you see how your proposition compares technically to alternatives.
2. Prioritising a product roadmap – Features are commonly used to describe elements of a product roadmap, which is the articulation of how your proposition could evolve over time.

When we think about features, the main challenge is to prioritise them. Should you add this feature to your proposition? If yes, when should you implement it?

> Should a chocolate brand wrap its chocolate bar in a biodegradable packaging?
>
> Should Microsoft Teams add the ability to hide your video on your screen without turning off your camera for the other participants?
>
> Should an e-commerce website implement the Facebook pixel that allows to track the performance of ads on Facebook and Instagram?

Developing new features comes at a cost. It's necessary to make sure that a new feature will create value for your audience and for your company too.

Prioritisation

There are three areas you need to look at when you are in the process of **prioritising** features:

1. **Desirability** is a marketing question. This is the focus of the Value Mix. Will the feature help your audience better achieve their goals? Will it fit with their beliefs? Is it something they will be willing to pay for?
2. **Feasibility** is a technical question. Can it be done? Is it legal? How long will it take to implement it? At what cost? These are questions for engineers, lawyers, industry experts, and tech partners.
3. **Viability** is a financial and strategic consideration. Your proposition has to be considered as a part of the overall business. Will it be profitable? Does it make sense for your organisation to do it? Is it aligned with your strategy? Adding a new feature creates additional costs (e.g., implementation cost and opportunity cost), so will it generate enough revenue to balance these costs?

Prioritisation looks like this Venn diagram:

Venn diagram for prioritising features

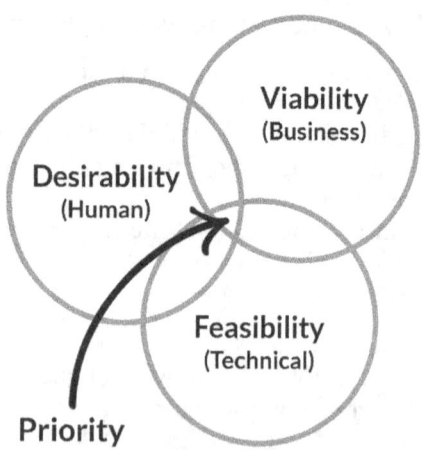

The prioritised features need to be desirable, viable, and feasible.

> **Key questions about your proposition:**
> What's the priority for your target audience? What are the must-haves? What is just nice to have?

Benefit: Definition

> *"People don't buy what you do; they buy how you make them feel."*
>
> — BERNADETTE JIWA, *Branding expert*

Benefits are the reasons (*logical and emotional*) that push your audience to buy your proposition. They tell your audience how your product or service creates value and what's in it for them.

A benefit is the outcome of a feature (or a set of features). You can use a simple formula to see how they relate to each other:

"A [*feature*], so that a [*benefit*]."

For example, the first iPod had [5GB] (*feature*), so that [you could have 1,000 songs your pocket] (*benefit*).

The benefit is the description of what a feature will mean to your audience:

- A laptop has a 10-inch screen, so that it's small and easy to carry around.
- A battery pack carries 5,200-mAh, so that you can fully charge your iPhone at least twice.
- A GoudronBlanc T-shirt is made with organic cotton, so that you can be proud of shopping more sustainably.

Having the right set of benefits will help to differentiate your proposition and make it stand out among the other alternatives.

A tool: The benefits ladder

Reframing features as benefits makes it easier for your audience to see how your proposition will improve their lives. But what could be difficult is to be relevant in the way you talk about each of the benefits.

The **benefits ladder** is a tool that helps you layer the emotional implication of a functional benefit. At the bottom, you get the feature. At the top, you get a series of emotional benefits.

To build a benefits ladder:

1. Pick a feature.
2. Think about what the feature means for the user. You must arrive at a quite functional benefit.
3. Repeat but this time using the benefit you just landed.
4. And then, repeat until you reach a benefit that seems too high level.

Most high-level benefits are about making people happier. What you need to find is the right level, i.e., a benefit that is emotional and tangible enough so it'll resonate with your audience.

Here's the example of a benefits ladder for an external phone charger:

The benefits ladder of an external charger

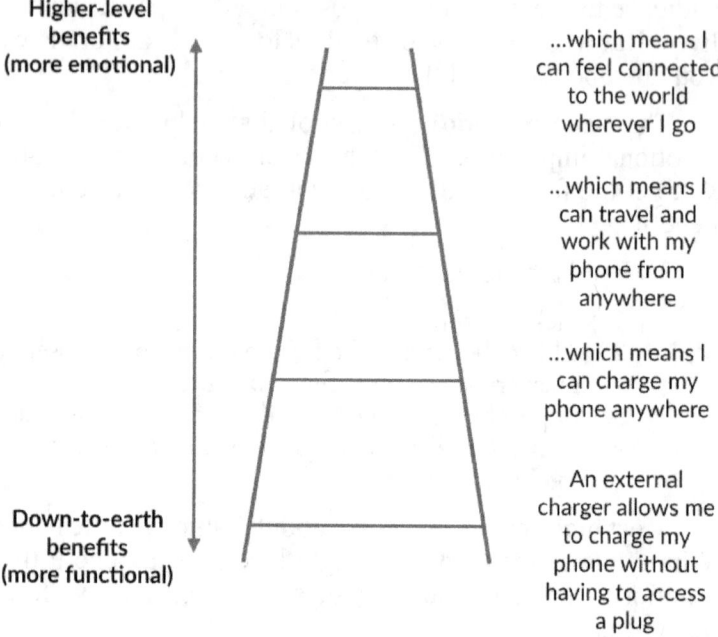

Higher-level benefits (more emotional)

...which means I can feel connected to the world wherever I go

...which means I can travel and work with my phone from anywhere

...which means I can charge my phone anywhere

An external charger allows me to charge my phone without having to access a plug

Down-to-earth benefits (more functional)

Key questions about your proposition:

What's in it for them? Why should they care about your proposition? How does your proposition help them achieve their goals?

Marketing question: Feature or Benefit?

You may have heard that your audience is more interested in the benefits than the features.

Indeed, benefits are the outcome of a feature (or set of features). They give your audience reasons to buy, since knowing the benefits tells them how your proposition can help them achieve their goals.

But sometimes, it's easier to talk about features to communicate how your proposition can help your audience.

It's the case when the audience is familiar with what a specific feature means for them.

- If I tell you "my iPhone has 8GB of memory", I can feel your compassion. Indeed, 8GB means that I am not able to store many photos, apps, and podcasts on my phone.
- If a store claims "open 24h", you know what it means. The store manager doesn't need to specify: "You can even come to our supermarket if you're running out of milk in the middle of the night."
- If you rent an "automatic" car, you know how it'll feel to drive it. There's no need to explain that you won't have to change gears and that the car does it automatically.
- If you buy 0% fat yogurt, you understand it'll be less heavy than the 5% fat version. You don't need to get it as "good to stay fit".

When the features are obvious, it can be more effective to let your audience make the jump to thinking about what it means for them rather than tell them about the benefits.

CHAPTER NINE:

Positioning

It's not just about the soda

In 1985, The Coca-Cola Company introduced what is known as the "new Coke".

At the time, consumer preference for Coca-Cola was reported to be in decline. Blind tastes showed that Americans seemed to prefer the taste of Pepsi Cola. So, The Coca-Cola Company decided to improve the formula of Coke. They replaced it with a formula called the "new Coke", which was chosen as the best alternative in taste tests by nearly 200,000 consumers.

But the launch of the new formula didn't go as expected. It led an unprecedented outcry in the US.

According to the Time, the company received over 40,000 letters of complaint and was flooded with phone calls and bad press. Three months later, they felt compelled to reintroduce the Coca-Cola "classic".

The Coca-Cola executives didn't expect that their target audience didn't want a better taste.

Indeed... Americans were buying a drink, but also a story.

They wanted the legend of the secret original formula, the symbol of their childhood, the pride of being American, and the most known brand in the world.

Positioning: Definition

> *"The most important decision is how to position your product."*
>
> – DAVID OGILVY, *Founder of Ogilvy & Mather*

Your **positioning strategy** is the set of stories you tell to differentiate your proposition and make it stand out against the available alternatives.

When you go to a Lidl, you experience the "we pass the savings to our customers" stories that Lidl stands for.

The storefront typically displays ads showing big discounts. In the shop, prices are surprisingly low. Most products are on shelves in their secondary packaging. The products are of good quality. And when you leave the store, you're offered a catalogue that features all the discounts that will be available the following week.

Everything is done to make the price-sensitive consumers feel that "it's like the same as in other supermarkets, but it's much cheaper".

Simply put, a positioning strategy creates a frame of reference that helps your audience understand what makes your proposition different and better *for* them.

It answers the question: "What is your proposition famous for?" And the answer must stick in people's minds.

Noticed vs. Unnoticed

> *"It's tricky to define better. But without a doubt, the heart and soul of a thriving enterprise is the irrational pursuit of becoming irresistible.*
>
> – SETH GODIN, *Author of This Is Marketing*

In a world where everything is one click away on Google, everyone wants to feel that they got the best and most relevant proposition.

You wouldn't like using a razor that is the second-best at making at a "baby butt smooth" shave. Or you wouldn't that your online shop is powered by the second-best e-commerce management system.

In today's world of unlimited choice and supply, getting noticed and standing out for being the most relevant alternative is critical. It's what will decide between the success or failure of your proposition.

You need a positioning strategy that makes your audience emotionally get how different your proposition is from the other alternatives and why it's so much better for them than the rest.

It shouldn't be the second-best. It should be seen as the best, and the most exciting and relevant option *for* them.

Positioning is perception

> *"Positioning is how you differentiate your brand in the mind. Positioning focuses on the perceptions of the prospect."*
>
> – AL RIES, *Author of Positioning*

The positioning of your proposition is based on **perception**, not facts. What matters is what *your audience* believes to be true, not what *you* think is true.

There's always a gap between what a customer thinks

about a proposition and what the company wants them to think. Your positioning strategy isn't the same as your brand.

> Your positioning strategy is your attempt to influence your audience so that your proposition stands out in their eyes and is recognised as different, better, and more relevant than the other alternatives.
>
> Your brand isn't what you say it is. It's what your audience feels and believes about your proposition and the value it creates for them.

Positioning is about perception, but your positioning strategy has to be **authentic**. It isn't about lying. The stories you tell must be aligned with the customer experience you create.

Your audience needs a reason to believe your stories. This could be scientific evidence, product features, the founders' reputation, having famous customers, the company's heritage, what their friends are saying, celebrity endorsement, or any iconic element that supports your positioning strategy.

It's one thing to claim that your brand sells the most remarkable yoga clothes. It's another to claim it while showing that some of the most well-known yoga teachers use your products.

Positioning is about your audience

As I mentioned before, the image of your proposition depends on the perception of your audience. Your positioning strategy must be something *they* would find relevant and would like to believe.

> GoPro targets people who have a bias towards extreme sport and see themselves as adrenaline junkies.
>
> Red Bull focuses on people who believe that a beverage can help them go through the day and be better at what they do.
>
> Lidl appeals to consumers who tend to be more price-sensitive, and don't want to put a fortune in grocery shopping.
>
> Nespresso wants to be the choice of people who enjoy the taste of good coffee, but don't want to go through the hassle of becoming a barista at home.

The stories you tell must reinforce your audience's worldviews, but they should also position your proposition as being the most exciting and relevant in their context and to the goals they are trying to achieve.

These stories should alleviate their concern, and make your proposition stand out among the other available alternatives.

You must start seeing how the "audience" side of the Value Mix framework fits with the "proposition". Creating your positioning strategy requires to do a lot of research to understand your audience at a deeper level.

Positioning is putting things in boxes

As human beings, we tend to put things and people in boxes. It's our way of making sense of the world.

Boxes are patterns we've learnt to recognised based on our biases, beliefs, and experience of the world (*worldviews*). Putting things in boxes helps our brain know what to expect.

We do this with people. Who doesn't have a friend or family member who is considered as being "the funny one" or "the lazy one"?

But we also do the same with brands and propositions. Your positioning strategy isn't just a slogan or a logo. It's a system of stories and iconic elements that you use to help your audience put your proposition in the right box.

And not everyone shares the same worldviews. Different audiences will put your proposition in different boxes.

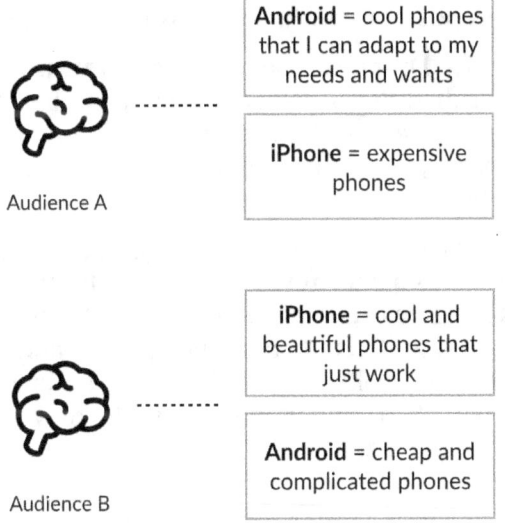

One group of people see iPhones as expensive phones, while another group will believe that iPhones are cool and beautiful phones that just work. Inversely, Android phones can be considered as a symbol of technological freedom by one group and cheap and complicated by another group.

Positioning must be laser-focused

> *"I could have positioned Dove as a detergent bar for men with dirty hands, but chose instead to position it as a toilet bar for women with dry skin. This is still working 25 years later."*
>
> – DAVID OGILVY, *Founder of Ogilvy & Mather*

Defining the positioning of your proposition is about making choices. It requires to choose what you want your proposition to be famous for and to know to whom you should say, "yes, this is for you" and more importantly, "no, this proposition isn't for you".

Focus is at the heart of positioning. It's about identifying the one or two things that are the most relevant for your audience, that are easy to understand and remember, and that can be explained quickly to other people.

Your proposition can't be famous for too many things.

In 2017, Dropbox launched a software aimed for businesses called Paper. When the company launched Paper, it described the software as "one part online document, one part collaboration, one part task management tool, one part content hub".

This is an example of a lack of focused positioning. If you search "dropbox paper review" on Google, you'll see how reviewers struggle to articulate what the software is for, whom it's for, and how it stands out among the other alternatives. The result? The makes it hard for the IT department of a company to explain to their colleagues why they should use it.

Positioning isn't just advertising

"The only thing that matters is everything."

– *DAVID HIEATT, Founder of Hiut Denim Co*

The positioning strategy for your proposition isn't just what you claim on an ad or a website. It's everything that shapes your proposition is perceived.

It's what the packaging looks like. It's how you make your audience feel when they buy and use your proposition. It's what they heard from their brother-in-law. It's what they see when they google the brand name. It's how your customer service team treats them. It's what influencers say about it.

It's also the iconic elements that stick in their minds when they think about your brand or your product category.

> It's the red sole of the Louboutin shoes.
> It's the orange boxes of Hermès.
> It's the bouncing lamp at the start of a Pixar movie.
> It's the no-frills seats of a Ryanair airplane.
> It's the shoes given to charity when you buy a pair of TOMS shoes.
> It's the way sales associates welcome you at the cashier of a Trader Joe's.
> It's your name on the cup you got at a Starbucks, even if it's sometimes misspelt.

Your positioning strategy is based on the stories you tell through copywriting, iconic elements, and customer experience. Your brand is how all of these make them feel.

Positioning helps you make decisions

> *"Everyone in the organisation should understand the brand positioning and use it as context for making decisions."*
>
> – *DAVID OGILVY, Founder of Ogilvy & Mather*

Your positioning strategy should be a North Star. It helps you and your team to make decisions about how to develop, sell, and improve your proposition. It's an organising framework that makes it easier to know what to do and what not to do.

When Apple decided to stand for "privacy", everyone in the organisation embraced the new positioning strategy.

The CEO talks publicly about privacy. The marketing team displayed the message "What happens on your iPhone, stays on your iPhone." on a massive advertising board in Las Vegas during the CES 2019. The product team implements features that protect privacy on your iPhone. The Intelligent Tracking Prevention of Safari stops advertisers from following you from site to site. Unlike other navigation apps, the Maps app doesn't keep a history of where you've been.

Every employee plays a role in making the positioning real and translating it into how customers perceive the proposition. Everyone from the CEO to the frontline should be aligned on the positioning strategy.

Key questions about your proposition:

What should your proposition be famous for? What do you want your audience to feel and believe? What do you want them to tell their friends?

CHAPTER TEN:

Customer Experience + User Experience

A perfect day to go to IKEA

Imagine… You're in your twenties and you're moving into an unfurnished flat (*context*).

Your reflex? "I should go to IKEA to get some stuff."

Now your challenge is to find how to get there. You need to find a friend who has a car or rent one to reach an Ikea store and bring back your purchase.

Once there, you go through an endless showroom. It feels like being in a museum. You choose the furniture you want. And, towards the end of the labyrinth, you pick up a few things for the kitchen. Then, you arrive in a warehouse where you have to find the furniture you selected. You put everything on a trolley. You pay and wonder whether you should get it delivered. But actually, it'll be more expensive and could take too much time. So, you try to fit everything in your friend's car (*customer experience*).

Back home, you're facing your next challenge. You now have to understand the user manuals to build your own furniture. Once it's done, you're ready to invite your friends for dinner to show your newly furbished flat (*user experience*).

Though some elements may feel clunky, IKEA designed a perfect customer experience for what you wanted: getting affordable pieces of furniture that look good and do not empty your bank account (*goal and worldview*).

Customer Experience: Definition

"In the factory we make cosmetics; in the drugstore we sell hope."

– CHARLES REVSON, Co-founder of Revlon

Your **customer experience** (CX) is how your proposition shows up in the life of your audience.

All the interactions before and after purchasing your proposition are part of the customer experience. It goes from your ads to the shopping experience to the experience of using your proposition and talking about it with other users.

These are all the moments where you can delight your audience to build loyalty and encourage them to share their experience and recommend your proposition.

The customer experience isn't just about a product. It's how you create value and deliver it to your audience. It's how you make them feel. It's the embodiment of your positioning strategy.

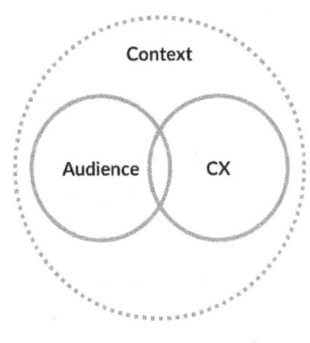

Keep in mind that people do not buy a pile of features. They buy stories and experiences, which are designed to help them achieve the goals that arise in particular contexts, to reinforce their worldviews, and to alleviate their concerns, while doing all of these better and in more exciting and relevant ways than the other available alternatives.

Make it remarkable

To keep running, a business must create a customer experience that consistently delivers at least what its customers expect to get, i.e., no bad surprises.

When you go to a coffee shop to grab a coffee with a friend, you expect a convenient location, good coffee, a clean space, and someone nice on the other side of the counter.

This is the bare minimum for a coffee shop.

But this isn't what will push you to tell all your friends about this coffee shop. It just feels like any other coffee shop.

To be worth talking about, the customer experience must also create a little something that is **remarkable**. It should create something that makes you feel great and that is worth talking about.

Doing something slightly better than the other alternatives isn't enough to stand out. Think about it as two levels of customer experience:

1. **Good** is about creating enough value so that someone is going to try your proposition.
2. **Great** is about creating such a remarkable customer experience that someone who tried your proposition is going to tell their friends about it.

Being remarkable is about creating and delivering value beyond what's expected. It's about offering the most relevant alternative, but also the most exciting one.

Key questions about your proposition:

How will your proposition show up in the lives of your customers? What will make your customer experience remarkable? What will make it worth talking about?

User Experience: Definition

The **user experience** (UX) is the moment of consumption or use of your proposition.

It's a component of the customer experience. It's a key moment that will influence whether your user will come back to buy again, and whether they will recommend your proposition to others.

There's something to keep in mind. The user and the customer can be two different persons. A user doesn't always decide to buy the proposition. This is especially the case in two situations:

1. In B to B, the user of Microsoft Teams didn't decide to use it. This is the IT department that decided that all the employees of a company will have to use Teams for collaboration.
2. When someone receives a gift, they may or may not have decided on the gift. And for sure, they didn't pay for it. But this is why the user may have received a jumper that is too small or a toy that isn't exactly the Playmobil they wanted.

Though the idea of user experience comes from the tech world, it is also applicable to consumer goods. Think about the experience of using a notebook, having a chocolate bar, charging your electric car, or eating at a restaurant.

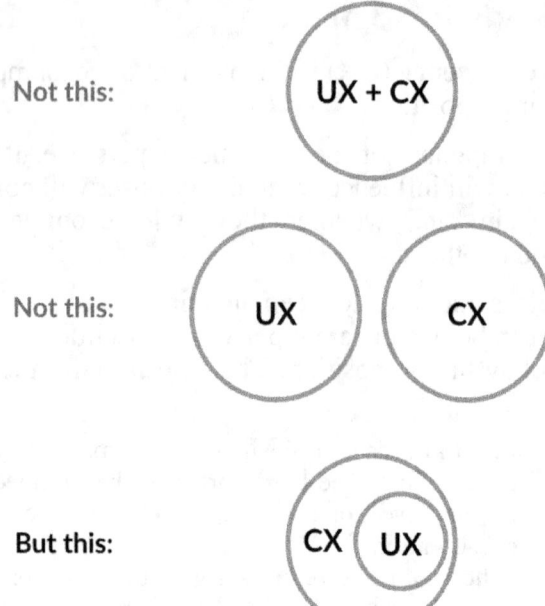

Evaluating the User Experience

To help you measure how relevant the user experience is, you can break it down into two attributes: "usefulness" and "usability".

1. **Usefulness** is about whether your proposition helps your audience achieve their goals. If a proposition is **not useful,** then, what's the point?
2. **Usability** is how easy and pleasant the user experience is for the user. If a proposition is **not easy to use,** the value your audience gets out it is limited by the friction created through the clunky user experience.

To stand out, the user experience needs one more thing. It needs "excitement".

3. **Excitement** is about providing a remarkable experience. It's making something happen that is worth talking about.

To create value for your audience, your proposition must be relevant, which requires both usefulness and usability. But it must also be exciting, making your audience feel great while using your proposition.

Key questions about your proposition:

How will they use your proposition? Will it be useful and easy to use? How exciting will it be?

Over to you!

I wrote this at the beginning of the book:

> *"The Value Mix aims to make it easier for you to think about the nuances of creating products and services that people will want, i.e., creating value for them."*

I really hope this book will help you to understand your audience at a deeper level and inspire you to find new ways to create value for them.

The ideal result would be if you end up launching a new proposition using the Value Mix.

Another great outcome would be if the framework helps you align with your team and partners when you run market research or work on creating new propositions.

The thinking that is at the foundation of the Value Mix has helped me create GoudronBlanc and delight thousands of customers around the world.

I honestly hope that this book will also help you build a stronger, better business that will find new ways to create value in our world.

Over to you, now!

Your Audience	Your Proposition
Worldviews	Customer Exp. / Positioning
Goals	+
Concerns	User Exp. / Features + Benefits
Context	Alternatives

ABOUT THE AUTHOR

Since 2016, Guerric de Ternay has led innovation projects at ?What If! part of Accenture Innovation, where he helps Fortune 500 companies spot opportunities for growth and invent new products and services.

Guerric is also the founder of GoudronBlanc, a menswear brand that makes high-quality T-shirts that men love to wear.

In 2018, he published *The Value Mix*, a book about creating products that people want, and he released a new edition in 2021. A year later, he published a second book called *The Opportunity Lenses*, which focuses on using foresight thinking to identify the most promising market opportunities to grow a business.

In 2024, Guerric published *The Inspiring Team Lead* with the ambition to help team leads and aspiring managers to build a positive team dynamic and inspire their team members to achieve unparalleled success.

A graduate of London Business School, Guerric also went to law school in Paris.

Find out more about his latest reflections at Guerric.co.uk

Subscribe to get more tips

I'm already thinking about the next book I want to work on. I'd love to keep in touch with you and let you know about what's next.

I'm looking forward to sharing my future work with you.

Also, I'm currently exploring the world of team-building activities. These are interesting techniques to energise your team in a meeting and add more adventure to your project.

I would like to give you a sneak peek by sharing my curated list of 7 effective team-building activities for your next meeting. These are straightforward, tried and tested methods that can make your next meeting more engaging and productive.

To get access to my list of effective team-building activities and the latest on what I publish, go to Guerric.co.uk/sneak-peek. Or scan the QR code below.

www.ingramcontent.com/pod-product-compliance
Lightning Source LLC
Chambersburg PA
CBHW071447220526
45472CB00003B/708